A Classical Chinese reader

A Classical Chinese reader

The Han shu biography of Huo Guang, with notes and glosses for students

Donald B. Wagner

CURZON

First published in 1998
by Curzon Press
15 The Quadrant
Richmond, Surrey, TW9 1BP

Typeset by Donald B. Wagner
Printed in Great Britain by
Biddles Limited, Guildford and King's Lynn

British Library Cataloguing in Publication Data
A catalogue record for this book is available from the British Library

Library of Congress in Publication Data
A catalogue record for this book has been requested

ISBN 0–7007–0960–6 (hbk)
ISBN 0–7007–0961–4 (pbk)

For Birthe Arendrup

Table of contents

Introduction

My hope for this book is that it will provide help to students making the transition from "textbook texts" to "real texts". Introductory textbooks of Classical Chinese naturally use texts which do not present serious philological problems, and whose understanding does not depend on a detailed knowledge of their historical context. Students beginning their own research therefore often find themselves at a loss reading "real" texts, in which such problems abound. This textbook uses a significant historical text, and all of the problems which it presents are confronted in the glosses and notes.

The text used here is the biography of Huò Guāng 霍光 in the *Hàn shū* 漢書, together with the commentaries compiled by Yán Shīgǔ 顏師古 (A.D. 541–645). Glosses are given for most unfamiliar words and phrases, and notes are provided on grammatical matters and on the historical context. Most of the glosses are translated directly from Chinese and Japanese dictionaries, and the source of each is indicated. It should be encouraging to see that one can arrive at a useful understanding of a significant historical text using standard reference works, without the help of an erudite Chinese master – though of course those who have such a master will always have the advantage over those who do not.

Advice to the student

Background reading. We are concerned here with a historical text, and in reading it you will need to know something of the history, culture, and institutions of the Hàn dynasty. Reading or re-reading the chapter on the Hàn period in any general work on Chinese history, whichever one you are already familiar with, should provide an adequate (though minimal) background as you start on the textbook. If you are at all interested in early Chinese history, however, you will want to read more. An excellent broad introduction to Hàn history is:

Pirazzoli-t'Serstevens, Michèle
The Han Dynasty, tr. by Janet Seligman. New York: Rizzoli, 1982. Also published with the title *The Han culture of China*. Orig. *La Chine des Han*, 1982.

Before reading further in the research literature on Hàn history it will be important to be familiar with the historical sources for the period. The most important of these are the three Official Histories (*Zhèng shǐ* 正史):

Shǐ jì 史記 (Records of the historian), by Sīmǎ Qiān 司馬遷 (ca. 145–90 B.C.) and his father Sīmǎ Tán 司馬談. A history of the known world from the beginnings to the authors' own time, thus incorporating approximately the first century of the Hàn period.

Hàn shū 漢書 (The book of Hàn), by Bān Gù 班固 (A.D. 32–92), his sister Bān Zhāo 班昭, and others. A history of China from the beginning of the Hàn to the period of the usurper Wáng Măng 王莽, i.e. from 206 B.C. to A.D. 25. For the first century of the Hàn it overlaps with the *Shǐ jì*, and in these parts the *Hàn shū* text is usually copied from the *Shǐ jì*, slightly rewritten.

Hòu Hàn shū 後漢書 (The book of Later Hàn), by Fàn Yè 范曄 (A.D. 398–445). A history of China from the Wáng Măng period to the final fall of the dynasty, i.e. from about A.D. 25 to 220. In writing this history Fàn Yè drew on a number of earlier histories of the same period, many of which had this same title, *Hòu Hàn shū*, which have survived only in part.

There is a vast literature available on these works, of which the following may be mentioned as some of the best:

Watson, Burton
Ssu-ma Ch'ien, Grand Historian of China. New York: Columbia University Press, 1958.

Chavannes, Édouard (tr.)
Les mémoires historiques de Se-ma Ts'ien. T. 1, 1895; t. 2, 1897; t. 3, 1898; t. 4, 1901; t. 5, 1905; t. 1–5 repr. Paris: Maisonneuve, 1967. T. 6, ed. and completed by Paul Demiéville, Max Kaltenmark, & Timoteus Pokora, Paris: Maisonneuve, 1969.
"Introduction", t. 1, pp. i–ccxlix.

Van Der Sprenkel, O. B.
Pan Ku, Pan Piao, and the Han history. Canberra 1964.

Swann, Nancy Lee
Pan Chao: Foremost woman scholar of China. First century A.D. Background, ancestry, life, and writings of the most celebrated Chinese woman of letters. (1932). Repr. New York 1968.

Bielenstein, Hans
"The restoration of the Han dynasty: With prolegomena on the historiography of the *Hou Han shu*", *Bulletin of the Museum of Far Eastern Antiquities* 1954, **26**: 1–209.
"Text history", pp. 9–20; "Historiography", pp. 20–81.

Beck, B. J. Mansvelt
The treatises of Later Han: Their author, sources, contents and place in Chinese historiography. Leiden: E. J. Brill, 1990 (*Sinica Leidensia*, 21).

Much more important than any of the secondary literature, however, is to read the sources themselves, in translation at first and later in the original. The following translations from the *Shǐ jì* and *Hàn shū* seem to be the most useful for students:

Chavannes' translation of the *Shǐ jì*, cited above, covers the first 52 chapters, most of which are related to pre-Hàn periods and thus are of less importance here.

Watson, Burton (tr.)
Records of the Grand Historian of China: Translated from the Shi chi of Ssu-ma Ch'ien. 2 vols., New York & London: Columbia University Press, 1961.
Rev. and expanded ed., *Records of the Grand Historian: by Sima Qian*. 1993.
Translates most of the chapters of the *Shǐ jì* which relate to the Hàn period.

Watson, Burton (tr.)
Courtier and commoner in ancient China: Selections from the History of the Former Han by Pan Ku. New York & London: Columbia University Press, 1974.

Dubs, Homer H. (tr.)
The history of the Former Han Dynasty, by Pan Ku, a critical translation with annotations. Vols. 1–3, Baltimore: Waverly Press, 1938, 1944, 1955. Tr. of *juàn* 1–12 + 99 of *Hàn shū*. Further volumes were planned but never published.

Watson is justly famous for his highly readable translations of ancient Chinese texts, but he is criticised for the very sparing commentary and philological apparatus in his translations; Dubs' translations from the *Hàn shū* are much more "scholarly", but not at all easy to read.

Published translations from the *Hòu Hàn shū* are few, but one can indirectly read it in translation by reading translations from the *Zīzhì tōngjiàn* 資治通鑑. This book is a year-by-year history of China from the fifth century B.C. to the tenth century A.D., compiled by Sīmǎ Guāng 司馬光 (1019–1086) by a scissors-and-paste method from the sources available to him. Since the *Hòu Hàn shū* was very nearly his only source for the Later Hàn period, the following translations from the *Zīzhì tōngjiàn* can be useful to students as substitutes for translations from the *Hòu Hàn shū*:

DeCrespigny, Rafe (tr.)
The last of the Han: Being the chronicle of the years 181–220 A.D. as recorded in chapters 58–68 of the Tzu-chih t'ung-chien of Ssu-ma Kuang (Centre of Oriental Studies, *Monograph* 9). Canberra: Australian National University, 1969.

DeCrespigny, Rafe (tr.)
Emperor Huan and Emperor Ling: Being the chronicle of Later Han for the years 157 to 189 AD as recorded in chapters 54 to 59 of the Zizhi tongjian of Sima Guang (*Faculty of Asian Studies monographs: New series*, 12). 2 vols., Canberra: Australian National University, 1989.

Besides the Official Histories there are numerous other historical sources for Hàn history, of which the following are two of the best known:

Yán tiě lùn 鹽鐵論 (Discourses on salt and iron), by Huán Kuān 桓寬 (1st cent. B.C.). Report on a state conference on administrative and economic problems held in 81 B.C.

Huá yáng guó zhì 華陽國志 (Treatise on the states south of Mount Huá), by Cháng Qú 常璩 (4th cent. A.D.). A history and geography of the region of modern Sìchuān from the Hàn to the author's own time.

There are two partial translations of the *Yán tiě lùn*:

Gale, Esson M. (tr.)
Discourses on salt and iron: A debate on state control of commerce and industry in ancient China. Taipei: Ch'eng-wen, 1967. This is a combined facs. repr. of the Leiden 1931 tr. of chapters 1–19 and the tr. of chapters 20–28 in *Journal of the North China Branch of the Royal Asiatic Society*, 1934, **65**: 73–110.

Baudry–Weulersse, Delphine, Jean Levi, & Pierre Baudry (trs.)
Chine, an –81: Dispute sur le sel et le fer. Yantie lun. Présentation par Georges Walter. Seghers, Paris, 1978.

At the moment there is not much available in Western languages from or about the *Huá yáng guó zhì*, but an article by Harald Bøckmann is expected.

Extremely informative and reliable on books of the Hàn and before is:

Loewe, Michael (ed.)
Early Chinese texts: A bibliographical guide (*Early China special monograph series*, 2). Berkeley: Society for the Study of Early China and Institute of East Asian Studies, University of California, 1993.

After becoming familiar with the most important sources for Hàn history you will be prepared to begin reading the research literature on the period. The place to start is:

Twitchett, Denis & Loewe, Michael (eds.)
The Cambridge history of China. Vol. 1: *The Ch'in and Han empires, 221 B.C. – A.D. 220*. Cambridge University Press, 1986.

This book, 1000 pages without a single illustration, is intentionally and emphatically an old-fashioned history. You may not wish to read it, but you will certainly want to use it as a reference work. Either read it or browse through it, then go on to its bibliography. Consider especially works by B. J. Mansvelt Beck, Hans Bielenstein, Rafe DeCrespigny, Patricia Ebrey, A. F. P. Hulsewé, Michael Loewe, Henri Maspero, C. M. Wilbur, and L. S. Yang.

On the material culture and archaeology of the Hàn there is not as much available as one would like, but a certain amount can be gained from the following:

Pirazzoli-t'Serstevens, Michèle, *The Han dynasty*, cited earlier

Wáng Zhòngshū 王仲殊
Han civilization. Tr. by K. C. Chang a.o. New Haven & London: Yale University Press, 1982. Tr. of a series of lectures given in the U.S., later published in China: *Hàn dài kǎogǔxué gàishuō* 漢代考古學概説 (A survey of Han archaeology). Běijīng: Zhōnghuá Shūjú, 1984.

Dien, Albert E. (et al., eds.)
Chinese archaeological abstracts, vols. 2–4 (*Monumenta archaeologica*, vols. 9–11). 3 vols., Los Angeles: Institute of Archaeology, University of California, 1985.

Two more specialized works, by Hayashi Minao and Käthe Finsterbusch, will be mentioned further below.

Huò Guāng and his time. The text we are concerned with here is the biography in the *Hàn shū* of Huò Guāng 霍光 (d. 68 B.C.), the *de facto* holder of supreme power under two Emperors. Most of the relevant chapters of the *Hàn shū* can be found in English translation in the books by Watson and Dubs cited above.[1]

Two important books deal at length with our period:

Loewe, Michael
Crisis and conflict in Han China, 104 B.C. to A.D. 9. London: Allen & Unwin, 1974.

Liu Pak-yuen (Liào Bóyuán 廖伯源)
Les institutions politiques et la lutte pour le pouvoir au milieu de la dynastie des Han antérieurs (*Mémoires de l'Institut des Hautes Études Chinoises*, 15). Paris: Collège de France / Diffusion de Boccard, 1983.

Either of these books will be useful for the background to the events covered by Huò Guāng's biography, but the most interesting aspect is the comparison between the two. Broadly speaking, Michael Loewe follows the traditional Chinese view, that Huò Guāng was a faithful servant of the Emperors under whom he served, while Liu Pak-yuen sees him as a manipulator who usurped the legitimate powers of the Emperors. What is more, this disagreement is sustained in spite of the fact that the authors use the same sources (chiefly Huò Guāng's biography), and use them almost uncritically, believing virtually every word of the *Hàn shū*. I invite you to read both books and then, while reading the biography of Huò Guāng, consider how such different interpretations of the same text can be possible. This is not the place to give my own view, but I suggest that you consider whether the reason is perhaps to be sought in events and currents of thought of Bān Gù's own time.

In reading Hàn historical texts it is important to know something of Hàn bureaucracy and institutions. The following can help:

Loewe, Michael
"The orders of aristocratic rank of Han China", *T'oung-pao*, 1960, **48**.1/3: 97–174.

[1] The basic sources for the period have been translated into Swedish by Arvid Jongchell in *Huo Kuang och hans tid: Täxter ur Pan Ku's Ch'ien Han shu* (Göteborg: Elanders Boktryckeri, 1930). Jongchell translated all of the relevant chapters of the *Hàn shū*, then cut up and rearranged the translations to form a continuous text with almost no further comment. This "scissors-and-paste" method is no longer accepted as a way of writing history, but the book will nevertheless be of great value to any student of the Hàn who can read Swedish.

Wang Yü-ch'üan
"An outline of the central government of the Former Han dynasty", *Harvard journal of Asiatic studies*, 1949, **12**: 134–187.

Bielenstein, Hans
The bureaucracy of Han times. Cambridge University Press, 1980.

Hucker, Charles O.
A dictionary of official titles in Imperial China. Stanford University Press, 1985.

Dictionaries and reference works. The only good Chinese–English dictionary of Classical Chinese is:

Karlgren, Bernhard
"Grammata Serica recensa", *Bulletin of the Museum of Far Eastern Antiquities* (Stockholm) 1957, **29**: 1–332. Facs. repr. as a separate vol., Göteborg 1964.

It is however concerned only with single characters and only with usage in pre-Hàn texts, and is therefore of limited use here. It is often useful in attempting to determine the primary or original meaning of a word and, as will be discussed below, it is also useful in dealing with the *fǎnqiè* 反切 sound glosses given by commentators of the Six Dynasties and Táng periods.

Using "Grammata Serica recensa" can unfortunately be rather laborious. In the body of the work, characters with the same phonetic part are grouped together, and the phonetic parts are listed by radical in the index. To find 談, for example, it does not help to look under the character's own radical, 言, no. 149. Instead one looks up the phonetic part, 炎, under *its* radical, 火, no. 86. This is on p. 327 of the index, and one finds here the number 617. Group no. 617 is listed on p. 165, where 炎 is no. 617a and 談 is no. 617l. The definition for no. 617l, on p. 164, is "*id.* speak (Shï)." Here "Shï" (for *Shī jīng* 詩經) indicates Karlgren's source for this meaning; normally he indicates the earliest text in which the character is used with the given meaning. "*Id.*" means that the pronunciation is the same as that of the previous character, which in this case is given as "**d'âm* / *d'âm* / t'an". These are the reconstructed Archaic and Ancient pronunciations, followed by the Mandarin pronunciation. The transcription system used for the reconstructed pronunciations is explained on pp. 3–4. The transcription system used for the Mandarin pronunciation is Karlgren's own, but it resembles the Wade–Giles system, and is easy enough to understand. The Mandarin tone is not given, but can often be worked out from the reconstructed Ancient pronunciation using rules given by Karlgren on p. 5.

I continue trying to persuade students not to use Mathews' *Chinese–English dictionary* or Liang's *New practical Chinese–English dictionary* in reading Classical Chinese texts, but without much success. These are the only Chinese–English dictionaries which are even barely adequate for the purpose, but they really cannot be recommended. They mix up meanings from all periods from the most ancient to the most modern, giving no indication of period and no usage examples; and they are also very often simply wrong. This one is somewhat better:

Couvreur, F. S.
Dictionnaire classique de la langue chinoise. [3ème éd. 1911]. Repr. Taiwan, 1963.

However I do not recommend Couvreur either, for we now have excellent modern Chinese dictionaries of Classical Chinese that are definitely preferable to anything available in Western languages. Most of the Chinese dictionaries to be discussed below are concerned with Classical Chinese only, and give along with each definition one or more examples of usage.

For single characters the following are useful:

Gŭ Hànyŭ chángyòng zì zìdiăn 古漢語常用字字典.
Běijīng: Shāngwù Yìnshūguăn, 1979.

Shĭ Dōng 史東
Jiănmíng gŭ Hànyŭ cídiăn 簡明古漢語詞典. Kūnmíng: Yúnnán Rénmín Chūbănshè, 1985.

Qián Dàqún 錢大群 & Qín Zhìpèi 秦至沛
Wényán chángyòng bābăi zì tōngshì 文言常用八百字通釋 Nánjīng Dàxué Chūbănshè, 1987.

One of the first two should be your basic "first try" dictionary; the second is better, but is more difficult to find in bookstores than the first. The third includes only 800 characters, and therefore cannot be used alone, but it gives a wealth of information on the usage of each of the characters which it does include.

For grammatical particles the following are quite good:

Yáng Bójùn 楊伯峻 & Tián Shùshēng 田樹生 (eds.)
Wényán chángyòng xūcí 文言常用虛詞. Chángshā: Húnán Rénmín Chūbănshè, 1983. Repr. 1985.

Chángyòng wényán xūcí cídiăn 常用文言虛詞詞典.
Xī'ān: Shănxi Rénmín Chūbănshè, 1983. Repr. 1984.

Characteristic for all of the modern Chinese dictionaries listed so far are that they are small and fairly cheap, that they are concerned primarily with single characters (though a few of the most common character combinations are also included), and that characters generally must be looked up in their simplified forms, which can sometimes be a nuisance.

When such small dictionaries are not adequate, a different sort of dictionary is required. The next step is to look up the character or phrase in one of the medium-sized dictionaries:

Cí yuán 辭源.
Rev. ed., 4 vols., Běijīng: Shāngwù Yìnshūguăn, 1979.

Cí hǎi 辭海.
Rev. ed., 3 vols., Shànghǎi: Shànghǎi Císhū Chūbǎnshè, 1979. Suppl. vol. 增補本, 1983.

These are larger, less handy, and much more expensive than the dictionaries listed earlier, and they are also more difficult to obtain outside China. Both include both single characters and combinations of characters. *Cí yuán* is devoted entirely to Classical Chinese, while *Cí hǎi* has modern meanings as well (with the period clearly indicated). For most purposes I prefer *Cí yuán*, but *Cí hǎi* also has its uses; in particular it seems to be better on classical names of animals and plants.

Obviously these Chinese–Chinese dictionaries often give definitions which one cannot understand, and it is then necessary to look up one or more words in a Chinese–English dictionary of modern Chinese; there are several good ones, but it would take us too far afield to discuss them here.

For those who are at ease with Japanese there is a wide selection of medium-sized Chinese–Japanese classical dictionaries available, one of which is:

Kadokawa Kan–Wa chū jiten 角川漢和中辭典.
Tōkyō: Kadokawa Shoten, 1959. Many reprs.

This seems to have about as many entries as *Cí yuán*, but it does not give usage examples and is therefore less useful.

When the medium-sized dictionaries are not enough one must go on to the large dictionaries, and this will normally mean a trip to the library. Few students will want to own these dictionaries themselves, because they are expensive and take up a great deal of bookshelf space.

Hànyǔ dà cídiǎn 漢語大詞典.
12 vols. + index, Shànghǎi Císhū Chūbǎnshè, 1986–1994.

Morohashi Tetsuji 諸橋轍次
Dai Kan–Wa jiten 大漢和辭典. 13 vols., Tōkyō: Taishūkan, 1955–60. Facs. repr. n.p. (Táiwān), n.d.

Zhōngwén dà cídiǎn 中文大辭典.
("Encyclopedic dictionary of the Chinese language"). 40 vols., Táiběi: Zhōngguó Wénhuà Xuéyuàn Chūbǎnshè, 1962–68. Many reprs.

Hànyǔ dà cídiǎn is a marvellous dictionary, definitely the best we have for Classical Chinese, and for most purposes it supersedes Morohashi, which was once the standard. The present book was largely written before it had been completely published, however, and it will be seen that I have often used Morohashi for the glosses where today I would use *Hànyǔ dà cídiǎn*.

Morohashi's dictionary does however still have its uses. One does not have to be very good at Japanese to use it: perhaps one semester's university instruction would be enough. One looks up a word, finds a definition in Japanese, and looks this up in Nelson's *Japanese–English Character Dictionary* or in Kenkyūsha's *New Japanese–English Dictionary*, whichever is appropriate. It is only necessary to note that Morohashi uses pre-reform *kana*, which means that a word like こふ

(or 請ふ), which looks as if it should be pronounced *kofu*, is actually pronounced *kou*, and must be looked up as such in the Kenkyūsha dictionary. There is a useful table of the older kana combinations in Nelson's dictionary, pp. 1015–1016.

The *Zhōngwén dà cídiǎn* is said to be largely a translation of Morohashi. It appears to be full of typographical and other errors, and since the publication of *Hànyǔ dà cídiǎn* it is no longer recommended.

A person can be referred to in a classical text by several different names, and this can sometimes give problems. The fastest way of dealing with alternate names is to look them up in the indexes to personal names in the three Hàn histories:

Zhōng Huá 鍾華 (comp.)
Shǐ jì rénmíng suǒyǐn 史記人名索引. Běijīng: Zhōnghuá Shūjú, 1977.

Wèi Liánkē 魏連科 (comp.)
Hàn shū rénmíng suǒyǐn 漢書人名索引. Běijīng: Zhōnghuá Shūjú, 1979.

Lǐ Yùmín 李裕民 (comp.)
Hòu Hàn shū rénmíng suǒyǐn 後漢書人名索引. Běijīng: Zhōnghuá Shūjú, 1979.

In the *Hàn shū* index, for example, one can look up Bólù Hóu 博陸侯, "the Marquis of Bólù", and find (on p. 222), that three men are referred to in the *Hàn shū* by this title: Huò Guāng 霍光, Huò Yǔ 霍禹, and Huò Yáng 霍陽. (Huò Yǔ was Huò Guāng's son and Huò Yáng was the great-grandson of a cousin.) Under Huò Guāng (on p. 52) we find a list of the names by which he is referred to in the *Hàn shū*: Huò Zǐmèng 霍子孟, Bólù Hóu 博陸侯, Bólù Xuānchéng Hóu 博陸宣成侯, and Huò jiāngjūn 霍將軍.

Of course every personal name used in this text will be found in the *Hàn shū* index. Even when reading other texts, however, these indexes will be useful, for the greater part of all the persons known at all from the Hàn are mentioned in one or another of the Hàn histories. Failing that, one can try *Cí yuán*, *Cí hǎi*, and Morohashi (there are no personal or place names in *Hànyǔ dà cídiǎn*). Often help can also be obtained from *Zhōngguó rénmíng dà cídiǎn* 中國人名大辭典 (orig. 1921, numerous reprints), but it pays to be wary of mistakes and typographical errors in this book.

In dealing with the technical terms of Chinese administration the following can be used:

Bielenstein, Hans
The bureaucracy of Han times. Cambridge University Press, 1980.

Hucker, Charles O.
A dictionary of official titles in Imperial China. Stanford University Press, 1985.

In talking and writing about Hàn history we need to have an agreed standard set of translations for official titles. Until recently the *de facto* standard was that used by Dubs in his translation (cited above); Bielenstein uses Dubs's translations and where necessary creates new translations after the same pattern. Since translations of official titles are in any case arbitrary, it would have been sensible to stick to one standard, but now we are in the unfortunate situation of having *three* competing sets of translations: Hucker has created a completely different set of translations, and the *Cambridge history of China* uses still another set. Whether one set of translations will in time win out as a new standard, and if so which, is impossible to predict today: I continue to use those of Dubs and Bielenstein, but am aware that the other two have their good points.

For a great many glosses concerning material objects the place to go is:

Hayashi Minao 林巳奈夫
Kandai no bunbutsu 漢代の文物. Kyōto Daigaku Jinbun Kagaku Kenkyūsho 京都大學人文科學研究所, 1976.

It is not necessary to know Japanese to use this book, though one can get much more out of it if one does. If for example one finds in a Hàn text a reference to a weapon called a *gǒuràng* 鉤鑲 one can look it up in the glossary (p. 586) and find references to p. 462 and figures 10-50 and 10-51. On p. 462 is a short description in Japanese of the *gǒuràng*, with a quotation in Chinese of a Hàn text which describes it and a reference (through item 375 on p. 574) to an article about it in a Chinese archaeological journal. Figure 10-50 is a sketch of an actual *gǒuràng* found in a Hàn grave, and figure 10-51 is a sketch of a Hàn tomb-relief showing a *gǒuràng* in use.

Further help in dealing with references to material objects can be found in:

Finsterbusch, Käthe
Verzeichnis und Motivindex der Han-Darstellungen. Bd. 1: *Text*, 1966. Bd. 2: *Abbildungen und Addenda*, 1971. Wiesbaden: Otto Harrassowitz.

Here one can find Hàn illustrations of a crossbow or a flute (by looking in the index under *Armbrust* or *Flöte*, pp. 200, 210) or indeed even a *gǒuràng* (Wade-Giles *kou-jang*, here mistakenly transcribed *kou-hsiang*, p. 220).

This textbook

The text. Two versions of our text are reproduced here, from the Zhōnghuá Shūjú 中華書局 edition (pp. T3–T41) and from the edition of Wáng Xiānqiān 王先謙, *Hàn shū bǔzhù* 漢書補注 (pp. T43–T65):

Hàn shū 漢書.
Běijīng: Zhōnghuá Shūjú, 1962.

Wáng Xiānqiān 王先謙 (ed.)
Hàn shū bǔzhù 漢書補注. Chángshā: Xūshòu Táng 虛受堂, 1900. Facs. repr. 2 vols., Běijīng: Zhōnghuá Shūjú, 1983.

Both include Yán Shīgǔ's commentary, and Wáng Xiānqiān gives additional commentary. The Zhōnghuá Shūjú edition, being typeset and punctuated, is obviously the more convenient to read, and it will be used as the basic text here. Line numbers have been added for convenient reference.

In Wáng Xiānqiān's edition the commentary is printed as in all pre-modern editions: each comment is printed in smaller characters directly after the point in the main text to which it refers. He gives Yán Shīgǔ's comment, then adds his own, if any, preceded by 〔補注〕. In the Zhōnghuá Shūjú edition the comments are gathered in convenient groups and keyed to the text using numbers.

The Zhōnghuá Shūjú editors' text emendations are given as follows. A small character in parentheses is a character in Wáng Xiānqiān's edition which should be deleted, and a large character in brackets is a character not in that text which should be inserted. For example, in lines 7–8 (p. T3), we find: 光為奉(常)〔車〕都衛. This means that the character 常 in Wáng Xiānqiān's edition is to be replaced with the character 車. The editors' reasons for their emendations are given at the end of each chapter, in this case on p. T40 (p. 2968 of the original): three early editions have 車 in this passage. The conventions followed by the editors are given in their preface.

Yán Shīgǔ in his commentary quotes a number of earlier commentaries. Most of these are no longer extant, and what we know of them comes almost entirely from Yán Shīgǔ's preface. I give some of this information in the notes.

Yán Shīgǔ's commentary often indicates the pronunciation of individual characters using the *fǎnqiè* 反切 ("turning and cutting") system. Two characters are given, from which the reader is to use the initial consonants of the pronunciation of the first and the final part of the pronunciation of the second. A common error of beginners is to attempt to use the *modern* pronunciations of the two characters, which can give bizarre results. It is necessary to use the pronunciation of the time of the commentator: in this case the Táng period. Bernhard Karlgren has reconstructed this pronunciation, which he calls Ancient Chinese, in *Grammata Serica recensa* (cited above).

An example of the use of the *fǎnqiè* system is in comment no. 2 after line 16 (p. T4): 屬音之欲反, "The sound of 屬 is given by the *fǎn[qiè]* of *zhī* 之 and *yù* 欲." To use this one looks up *zhī* and *yù* in *Grammata Serica recensa* and finds their pronunciations in Ancient Chinese, respectively *tśi* and *i̯wok*. The initial part of the first is *tś-*, and the final part of the second is *i̯wok* (the whole syllable, because there is no initial consonant). Putting these together gives *tśi̯wok*. Now looking up 屬 in *Grammata Serica recensa*, one finds that the character has two meanings, with two different pronunciations:

> modern *shǔ*, Ancient *źi̯wok*, "be attached to"
> modern *zhǔ*, Ancient *tśi̯wok*, "to attach"

Yán Shīgǔ has thus told us which of these meanings the character has here, and such information can be very useful.

In my glosses I have included the Ancient pronunciation of every character involved in a *fǎnqiè* sound gloss. You will notice that the results are not always as straightforward as in the above example; such cases are matters for the linguists to worry about, and I have only rarely had anything to say about them.

The glosses. The gloss list gives definitions of words which are likely to be unfamiliar to students who have read no more than an introductory textbook such as Harold Shadick's *A first course in literary Chinese* (1968). The emphasis is on multi-character words (because single-character words are much easier to find in dictionaries) and on rare meanings for familiar words. In each case I have translated the definition from a Chinese or Japanese dictionary and added a reference to this source, using the abbreviations in the list below. There is very little system in my choice of which dictionary to use for any particular gloss: this book has grown with use, and my taste in dictionaries has changed over time.

I use certain conventions in the glosses. Distinctly different meanings are separated by semicolons. Three dots at the beginning of a definition indicate that I have omitted one or more familiar meanings and give only an unusual meaning, while three dots at the end of the definition indicate that I have omitted one or more meanings which I consider obscure and/or irrelevant. Occasionally it can be useful to know that a certain character combination is *not* found in a major dictionary; here this is indicated with the sign "\", so that for example "\CY" means "Not in *Cí yuán*".

Numbers in the left margin indicate the line number in which the word glossed occurs. An indication like "16.2" means "comment no. 2 after line 16".

As noted above, Karlgren's reconstruction of the Ancient Chinese pronunciation is given for all characters involved in *fǎnqiè* sound glosses in the commentary.

For each official title I include Bielenstein's translation, for example "General of Agile Cavalry" for *piàojì jiāngjūn* 票騎將軍 (line 1). Here and there I have also felt it necessary to quote what Bielenstein says about the rank and duties of the position, but in general interested students will have to go to Bielenstein's book to find out this sort of thing.

The pronunciations are taken from Chinese dictionaries, and where the dictionaries do not agree I have normally used the pronunciation given in the little *Xīnhuá zìdiǎn* 新華字典 (1979 and later reprints), which in the matter of pronunciations is prescriptive rather than descriptive. If you have a Chinese teacher you should of course follow his or her pronunciation – it is absolutely silly to argue about pronunciation with a native speaker, even when other native speakers disagree.

You will have to decide for yourself how important correct pronunciation is in a language like Classical Chinese, which you will never have occasion to speak. There is a particular problem here concerning what some *Western* Sinologists insist upon as correct. Many teachers tell their students that, in reading Classical Chinese, *bái* 白 is to be pronounced *bó*, *chē* 車 is to be pronounced *jū*, etc. These special pronunciations were learned by an early generation of Sinologists from their Chinese teachers. They are examples of a venerable tradition of *yán wén yì dú* 言文異讀, "different readings in speech and writing", which, curiously enough, seems to have been preserved only in the West. Very few of these variant readings are indicated in modern Chinese dictionaries, and as far as I have been able to determine, most scholars in China today (mainland, Táiwān, Hong Kong) neither use them nor have even heard of them. Many students, having laboriously learned that the "correct" pronunciation of the poet 李白's name is Lǐ Bó rather than Lǐ Bái, have had the embarrassing experience of being politely corrected by Chinese friends who find it odd that they should mispronounce such a common character. For linguists the *yán wén yì dú* tradition provides valuable historical evidence; the rest of us can, in my opinion, take an entirely pragmatic view of what is correct.

One may very well wonder where to stop in looking up character combinations in dictionaries. For example, was it really necessary to look up *qiúwèn* 求問 (in the glosses for line 4) in Morohashi's dictionary? The first character means "to seek", the second "to ask", and in context the combination clearly means "to inquire about". There are three remarks to make here. First, the mere fact that the combination is in Morohashi tells us that it was a commonly used word, and the characters are not to be translated separately, as something like "to seek and inquire". Second, Morohashi gives an example of the use of the combination, in this case from the *Shǐ jì*, and such examples can be very useful in understanding the use of the word in other texts. I have not felt that I had the time or the patience to include the usage examples in my definitions, though that would in principle have been a good thing to do, but students can check them out in the locations indicated. Finally, if for example in line 3 one translates the combination *guìxìng* 貴幸 according to the individual characters, as something like "honoured and fortunate", one will miss the whole point of the sentence in which it occurs, for this word means specifically to be favoured by a ruler. The only way to find out this sort of fact is to look up the word in a dictionary.

But having said all this, it is also necessary to note that dictionaries have their limits, and that one's time is limited. One needs an instinct for what is worth looking up, and perhaps this textbook will be of some help in developing such an instinct.

Uses for this textbook. Teachers have their teaching methods, and do not really want to be told their job, so I have nothing to say to them here. I hope, however, that the book will also prove useful in self-study, and in that context there are perhaps a few things to say.

Depending on your purposes, and on how advanced you are in Classical Chinese, you can choose to read either the modern typeset and punctuated edition (pp. T3–T41) or Wáng Xiānqiān's unpunctuated wood-block edition (pp. T43–T65). You can also choose to read Yán Shīgǔ's commentary or to ignore it. After you have been through the text, using the glosses and looking up whatever more you need, Burton Watson's translation (in *Courtier and commoner in ancient China*, cited above, pp. 121–157) will be very useful in checking your understanding.

When you have been through this book you will have a detailed understanding of a significant Hàn text, and will be able to use that understanding in any number of ways. You may for example look at it as a historical source, or a literary text, or a linguistic example, and analyse it as such. If you are primarily interested in improving your command of Classical Chinese, you will want to learn its vocabulary and its grammatical structures. We all have our ways of doing this, but one way that I and some of my students have found useful is to read the text aloud many times over. After reading and understanding a page or so, one places ten coins on the table and reads the text aloud ten times, taking a symbolic reward of one coin for each reading. —Reading *aloud* is important, for when reading silently it is too easy to "cheat". Most Chinese teachers would advise you to memorise large parts of the text, and what I suggest here is a lazy person's version of memorisation. Either way, this is a useful means of both learning vocabulary and becoming intimately familiar with the grammatical and rhetorical patterns of Classical Chinese.

A good way forward for more advanced self-study after this textbook would be to read some of the other chapters in the *Hàn shū* which touch in one way or another on the story of Huò Guāng. In reading these you will already know the historical background and also a certain amount of the vocabulary, so that the amount of dictionary work required will be less than in reading an unrelated text.

An obvious place to begin is the biography of Jīn Mìdī 金日磾, which follows directly after Huò Guāng's in *juàn* 68. It is reproduced here (pp. T31–T36), but I have not provided glosses or notes for it. Then there are the Annals of the two Emperors Huò Guāng served, Zhāo-dì 昭帝 and Xuān-dì 宣帝, *juàn* 7–8 of the *Hàn shū*, which have been translated by Dubs (cited above, vol. 2, pp. 151–175 and 199–265). For those who are seriously interested in Hàn history it will be important to read examples like these of *Hàn shū* Annals, but they are dry and disjointed, and many will prefer to continue reading biographies, for example *juàn* 63, the collective biography of the five sons of the emperor Wǔ-dì 武帝. This has been translated by Watson (*Courtier and commoner*, pp. 46–78, cited above).

. . .

This book owes a great deal to all the students who have worked with me over the years. There are several whom I would have liked to thank by name for their trenchant (sometimes caustic) comments, but the list became too long – in this place a collective anonymous thanks will have to suffice. All errors are mine.

A book like this is a heap of details, and I am heavily conscious of how many errors must remain. I hope teachers and students will share with me their experience in using the book, and inform me of errors to be corrected in a later edition.

Abbreviations

B	Bielenstein, Hans *The bureaucracy of Han times*. Cambridge University Press, 1980.
BB	Qián Dàqún 錢大群 & Qín Zhìpèi 秦至沛 *Wényán chángyòng bābǎi zì tōngshì* 文言常用八百字通釋. Nánjīng Dàxué Chūbǎnshè, 1987.
Cambridge History	*The Cambridge history of China, vol. 1: The Ch'in and Han empires, 221 B.C. – A.D. 220*. Cambridge University Press, 1986.
CH	*Cí hǎi* 辭海. Rev. ed., 3 vols., Shànghǎi: Shànghǎi Císhū Chūbǎnshè, 1979. Suppl. vol. 增補本, 1983.
Couvreur, *Tch'ouen ts'iou*	Couvreur, Séraphin (tr.) *Tch'oun ts'iou et Tso tchouan: Texte chinois avec traduction française*. 3 vols., Ho Kien Fou 河間府: Imprimerie de la Mission Catholique. Facs. repr. retitled *La chronique de la principauté de Lòu*, 3 vols., Paris: Cathasia, 1951.
CY	*Cí yuán* 辭源. Rev. ed., 4 vols., Běijīng: Shāngwù Yìnshūguǎn, 1979.
DM	Xiè Shòuchāng 謝壽昌 (et al., eds.) *Zhōngguó gǔjīn dìmíng dà cídiǎn* 中國古今地名大辭典. Shànghǎi: Shāngwù Yìnshūguǎn, 1931. Numerous reprs.
Dù liáng héng	*Zhōngguó gǔdài dù liáng héng tújí* 中國古代度量衡圖集. Běijīng: Wénwù Chūbǎnshè, 1984.
Dubs	Dubs, Homer H. (tr.) *The history of the Former Han Dynasty*, by Pan Ku, a critical translation with annotations. Vols. 1–3, Baltimore: Waverly Press, 1938, 1944, 1955.
GHY	*Gǔ Hànyǔ chángyòng zì zìdiǎn* 古漢語常用字字典. Běijīng: Shāngwù Yìnshūguǎn, 1979.
GSR	Karlgren, Bernhard "Grammata Serica recensa", *Bulletin of the Museum of Far Eastern Antiquities* (Stockholm) 1957, **29**: 1–332. Facs. repr. as a separate vol., Göteborg 1964.
Hàn shū	*Hàn shū* 漢書. Běijīng: Zhōnghuá Shūjú, 1962.

Hòu Hàn shū	*Hòu Hàn shū* 後漢書. (The history of the Later Hàn dynasty, A.D. 25–220, by Fàn Yè 范曄, 398–445). Shanghai: Zhonghua Shuju, 1965; repr. 1973.
Hucker	Hucker, Charles O. *A dictionary of official titles in Imperial China*. Stanford University Press, 1985.
HY	*Hànyŭ dà cídiăn* 漢語大詞典. 12 vols. + index, Shànghăi Císhū Chūbănshè, 1986–1994.
JM	Shĭ Dōng 史東 *Jiănmíng gŭ Hànyŭ cídiăn* 簡明古漢語詞典. Kœnmíng: Yúnnán Rénmín Chūbănshè, 1985.
Karlgren, ***Compendium***	Karlgren, Bernhard "Compendium of phonetics in Ancient and Archaic Chinese", *Bulletin of the Museum of Far Eastern Antiquities*, 1954 , **26**: 211–367.
Knechtges, ***Wen xuan 1***	Knechtges, David R. (tr.) *Wen xuan, or Selections of refined literature*. Vol. 1: *Rhapsodies on metropolises and capitals*. Princeton University Press, 1982.
KXZD	*Kāngxī zìdiăn* 康熙字典. Repr. Hong Kong: Zhōnghuá Shūjú, 1958.
Legge, ***Ch'un ts'ew***	Legge, James (tr.) *The Chinese classics: With a translation, critical and exegetical notes, prolegomena, and copious indexes*. Vol. 5, pts. 1–2: *The Ch'un ts'ew, with the Tso chuen.* Hongkong: Lane, Crawford; London: Trübner, 1872. Facs. repr. Hong Kong University Press, 1960.
Legge, ***Li ki***	Legge, James (tr.) *The sacred books of China. The texts of Confucianism, Parts III–IV: The Li ki*. London: Clarendon Press, 1885; facs. repr. Delhi: Motilal Banarsidass, 1966.
Legge, ***Shoo king***	Legge, James (tr.) *The Chinese classics: With a translation, critical and exegetical notes, prolegomena, and copious indexes*. Vol. 3, pts. 1–2: *The Shoo king.* Hong Kong: Legge; London: Trübner, 1865. Facs. repr. Hong Kong University Press, 1960.
Loewe, ***Crisis and conflict***	Loewe, Michael *Crisis and conflict in Han China, 104 B.C. to A.D. 9*. London: Allen & Unwin, 1974.
M	Morohashi Tetsuji 諸橋轍次 *Dai Kan–Wa jiten* 大漢和辭典. 13 vols., Tōkyō: Taishūkan, 1955–60. Facs. repr. n.p. (Táiwān), n.d.

Wáng Xiānqiān	Wáng Xiānqiān 王先謙 (ed.) *Hàn shū bǔzhù* 漢書補注. Chángshā: Xūshòu Táng 虛受堂, 1900. Facs. repr. 2 vols., Běijīng: Zhōnghuá Shūjú, 1983. NB: *juàn* 68 is reproduced here on pp. T43–T65.
Wáng Zhòngshū, *Han civilization*	Wang Zhongshu 王仲殊 *Han civilization.* Tr. by K. C. Chang a.o. New Haven & London: Yale University Press, 1982.
Watson, *Courtier and commoner*	Watson, Burton (tr.) *Courtier and commoner in ancient China: Selections from the History of the Former Han by Pan Ku.* New York & London: Columbia University Press, 1974.
Watson, *Records*	Watson, Burton (tr.) *Records of the Grand Historian: by Sima Qian.* New York & Hong Kong: Columbia University Press, 1993.
WYXC	Yáng Bójùn 楊伯峻 & Tián Shùshēng 田樹生 (eds.) *Wényán chángyòng xūcí* 文言常用虛詞. Chángshā: Húnán Rénmín Chūbǎnshè, 1983. Repr. 1985.

Notes and glosses

	金日磾	Jīn Mìdī	(This is the pronunciation according to CH 3875.2).
		Jīn Mītī	(This is the pronunciation according to CY 3164.3).
line 1	票騎將軍	*piàojì jiāng-jūn*	General of Agile Cavalry (B).
	霍去病	Huò Qùbìng	140–117 B.C. (CY 3339.2). He has biographies in *Shǐ jì* and *Hàn shū*; the *Shǐ jì* biography is translated in Watson, *Memoirs*, pp. 163–184.
	河東[郡]	Hédōng [jùn]	A Hàn commandery (CY 1754.1). North of modern Xiàxiàn 夏縣, Shānxī (DM 515.1). → line 290.
	平陽[縣]	Píngyáng [xiàn]	A Hàn prefecture near modern Línfén 臨汾, Shānxī (CY 994.1).

The Hàn empire was geographically divided into a number of large units normally designated *jùn* 郡, and each *jùn* was divided into a number of *xiàn* 縣. (The number of large units varied in the course of the dynasty between 57 and 103.) Bielenstein translates these terms "commandery" and "prefecture" respectively. If one of the large units was given as a fief to a king (*wáng* 王), it was called a *guó* 國, usually translated "kingdom". One of the larger *or* smaller units could be given as a fief to a marquis (*hóu* 侯), and be called a *hóuguó* 侯國, "marquisate". A *xiàn* was divided into *xiāng* 鄉 (translated "districts"), each *xiāng* into *tíng* 亭 ("communes"), and each *tíng* into *li* 里 ("hamlets"). A more general term for such sub-*xiàn* units was *jù* 聚 ("agglomeration"). (B, pp. 99–104).

	以	*yǐ*	. . . ; in the capacity of (BB).
	縣吏	*xiànlì*	Prefectural official (M 8: 1150.1).
	給事	*jǐshì*	To manage; to hold office; abbreviation of 給事中, official title (CY 2427.3). *Jǐshì zhōng* → line 56.
2	侍者	*shìzhě*	Court attendant; . . . (CY 204.3).

	私通	*sītōng*	Secret communications; secret sexual intercourse (M 8: 532).
	吏	*lì*	. . . ; to serve as an official (BB).
	娶婦	*qǔfù*	To take a wife (M 3: 716).
	久之	*jiǔzhī*	After a long time (JM).
3	女弟	*nǚdì*	Younger sister (CY 729.2).
	得幸	*déxìng*	Obtain the trust and affection of a superior; (esp., of a woman:) to obtain the favour of the Emperor (CY 1079.2).
	姊	*zǐ*	Elder sister; term of respect for a woman older than oneself (CY 747.1).
	貴幸	*guìxìng*	To have an honoured position and be intimate with the ruler (CY 2957.3).
	壯大	*zhuàngdà*	Youth; prime of life (M 3: 2561.3).
	自	*zì*	. . . ; begin (CY 2582.1).
4	求問	*qiúwèn*	To inquire about (M 6: 905.3).
	會	*huì*	. . . ; happen to be (JM).
	太守	*tàishǒu*	Grand Administrator (B).
	郊迎	*jiāoyíng*	Go outside the city wall to meet someone (in order to show respect) (CY 3101.2).
	傳舍	*zhuànshè*	Post station, hostel (CY 251.2, M 1: 905.3).
	遣	*qiǎn*	To send; . . . (GHY).
5	趨	*qū*	To go in haste; . . . (GHY).
	拜謁	*bàiyè*	Pay a formal visit (to a superior); . . . (HY 6:433).
	迎拜	*yíngbài*	To meet and do reverence to (M 11: 7).
	因	*yīn*	. . . ; while (WYXC).
	跪	*guì*	To kneel (GHY).
	不早	*bùzǎo*	\CY \HY

	遺體	*yítǐ*	(Ancient:) offspring; (modern:) corpse (CY 3091.3).
	扶服	*púfú*	Prostrate oneself (same as 匍匐) (CY 1215.3).
6	叩	*kòu*	To knock; . . . (GHY).
	叩頭	*kòutóu*	磕頭 to kowtow (GHY).
	託命	*tuōmìng*	To entrust one's fate to (CY 2878.1).
	天力	*tiānlì*	The strength of Heaven (HY 2: 1405).
	宅	*zhái*	Residence; place for settlement; . . . (GSR 780b).
	田宅	*tiánzhái*	Agricultural land and residential land (M 7: 1057.4).
7	郎	*láng*	Gentleman (B).
	稍	*shāo*	Gradually; slightly (GHY).
	諸曹侍中	*zhūcáo shì-zhōng*	\B
	曹	*cáo*	Bureau. "The office staff was organized into Bureaus which were the backbone of Han bureaucracy" (B, p. 8).
	侍中	*shìzhōng*	Palace Attendant (B). "Their role was to offer advice and guidance to the emperor, and to be ready with answers to sudden questions" (B, pp. 59–60).
	奉車都尉	*fèngchē dū-wèi*	Chief Commandant of Imperial Equipages (B). (B has *jū* for *chē*).
8	光祿大夫	*guānglù dà-fū*	Imperial Household Grandee (B).
	奉	*fèng*	To hold in both hands; to present; to receive respectfully; to respect, obey (laws etc.); term of respect; to provide; to support; an official's salary (GHY).
	奉車	*fèngchē*	官名 (CY 717.3, M 3: 581.3).
	闒	*tà*	Door, gate (GHY).

	禁闥	*jìntà*	Inside the Imperial Palace (CY 2283.1).
	謹慎	*jǐnshèn*	Careful and discreet (CY 2916.1).
	親信	*qīnxìn*	Intimacy and trust (CY 2857.3).

After line 9

9.1	仲	*zhòng*	Anc. *d̂'i̯ung-* (GSR 1007f)
	中	*zhōng* *zhòng*	Anc. *ȶi̯ung* Anc. *ȶi̯ung-* (GSR 1007a).
9.2	遣	*qiǎn*	→ line 4.
	供侍	*gōngshì*	To be employed, to serve (M 1: 756.4).
9.3	郊	*jiāo*	Area within 100 *lǐ* 里 outside the walls of a city (CY 3101).
	界	*jiè*	Border; area; . . . (GHY).
	郊界	*jiāojiè*	\CY \M \HY
9.4	蒲	*pú*	Anc. *b'uo* (GSR 102n')
	北	*běi*	Anc. *pək* (GSR 909a)
	服	*fú*	Anc. *b'iuk* dominate, subdue; . . . id. garment, robe (GSR 934d)
	匐	*fú* *bo*	Anc. *b'iuk*; Anc. *b'ək* (GSR 933m).
10	征和	Zhēnghé	Reign period, 92–89 B.C.
	江充	Jiāng Chōng	(See Watson, *Courtier and commoner*, pp. 47–50).
	王	*wáng*	(Zhōu:) ruler; (Hàn:) highest aristocratic rank (GHY). King (B).
	衛太子	Wèi tàizǐ	Crown Prince born of a woman surnamed Wèi. His name was Liú Jù 劉據, and he was a son of Wǔ-dì. See Watson, *Courtier and commoner*, pp. 46–54.

燕王旦	Yān wáng Dàn	Liú Dàn 劉旦, son of Emperor Wǔ-dì 武帝; see Watson, *Courtier and commoner*, pp. 54–65.
廣陵王胥	Guǎnglíng wáng Xū	Liú Xū 劉胥, son of Emperor Wǔ-dì 武帝; see Watson, *Courtier and commoner*, pp. 65–69.
過失	*guòshī*	mistake (CY 3078.3). CY quotes a commentator on the legal treatise of the *Jìn shū* 晉書: 不意誤犯曰過失.

The first sentence refers to the famous witchcraft affair of 91 B.C., in which members of the Wèi 衛 family were accused of using witchcraft against the Emperor. It ended in five days of fighting between the troops of the Crown Prince and those of the Emperor. See Loewe, *Crisis and conflict*, pp. 37 ff.

	寵姬	*chǒngjī*	Favourite concubine (M 3: 3386).
	鉤弋[宮]	Gōuyì [gōng]	(Name of a Hàn palace) (CY 3181.2).
11	倢伃	*jiéyú*	漢女官名 (CY 227.1). Favourite Beauty (B). "The Chinese, in their systematic fashion, also bureaucratized the harem" (B, p. 73). In the time of Wǔ-dì there were ten ranks for court ladies, of which *jiéyú* was the highest.
	嗣	*sì*	. . . ; successor (GHY).
	輔	*fǔ*	. . . ; to assist the Emperor (GHY).
	任大重	*rèn dà zhòng*	\CY \M
	任重	*rènzhòng*	To have heavy duties (M 1: 640).
	屬	*shǔ*	Be subordinate to; belong to; category; . . .
		zhǔ	Attach, connect; entrust to; give a charge to, order; . . . (GHY).
	社稷	*shèjì*	Altars of grain and soil; the State (GHY).
	黃門	*huángmén*	Yellow Gates. (They gave access to the private quarters of the Emperor and his women.) (B).
12	負	*fù*	To carry on the back; . . . (GHY). → lines 69, 111.

The five ranks of Zhōu 周 feudal aristocracy, with their commonest English translations:

gōng 公 "duke"
hóu 侯 "marquis"
bó 伯 "earl"
zǐ 子 "viscount"
nán 男 "baron"

	周公	Zhōu gōng	The Duke of Zhōu, regent of the infant King Chéng 成王 (trad. r. 1115–1077).
	朝	*cháo*	To attend in audience; to receive in audience; the court; . . .
		zhāo	. . . (GHY).
	諸侯	*zhūhóu*	A general designation for the lords of the feudal states which shared political power in ancient times. In the Zhōu there were five ranks [see above]; in the Hàn there were two: *wáng* 王 ["King"] and *hóu* 侯 ["Marquis"] (CY 2902.1).
	賜	*cì*	Bestow (on an inferior) (GHY).
	後元	Hòuyuán	Reign period, 88–86 B.C.
	五柞宮	Wǔzuò gōng	Palace of Five Oaks (CY 143.1, 1551.1). \B
	病篤	*bìngdǔ*	Illness becomes critical (GHY).
	涕泣	*tìqì*	To weep (CY 1791).
13	不諱	*bùhuì*	Euphemism for death (CY 72.1).
	當	*dāng*	. . . ; suitable, appropriate (GHY).
	諭	*yù*	. . . ; to understand (JM).
	少子	*shàozǐ*	Youngest son (CY 892.2).
	頓	*dùn*	To knock (head); stamp (foot); rectify; stop; abandon; destroy; . . . (JM).
	頓首	*dùnshǒu*	To knock the head, the second of the Nine Obeisances (*jiǔ bài* 九拜) in Zhōu ritual (CY 3387.2).

14	大司馬	*dàsīmǎ*	Commander-in-chief (B).
	大將軍	*dàjiāngjūn*	General-in-chief (B).
	車騎將軍	*chējì jiāngjūn*	General of Chariots and Cavalry (B). (B has *jū* for *chē*).
15	及	*jí*	Until; while; . . . (JM).
	太僕	*tàipú*	Grand Coachman (B).
	上官	Shàngguān	. . . ; surname (CY 60.1).
	左將軍	*zuǒ jiāngjūn*	General of the Left (B).
	搜粟都尉	*sōusù dūwèi*	Chief Commandant Who Searches for Grain. "No more is known about the duties of [this] official other than what can be deduced from his title, i.e. provisioning the army." (B, p. 44).
	桑弘羊	Sāng Hóngyáng	152–80 B.C. See Cambridge History, esp. pp. 562–3.
	御史大夫	*yùshǐ dàfū*	Grandee Secretary (B).
	拜	*bài*	. . . ; appoint to a position (GHY).
	臥內	*wònèi*	Bedroom (CY 2577.3).
	牀	*chuáng*	Bed (= 床) (GHY).
	遺詔	*yízhào*	Deathbed decree of a ruler (M 11: 185).
16	少主	*shàozhǔ*	A young ruler (M 4: 3495).
	崩	*bēng*	. . . ; (of a ruler:) to die (GHY).
	襲	*xí*	. . . ; to succeed (to a throne. etc.) (GHY).
	尊號	*zūnhào*	Honorific term of address for Emperor or Empress (CY 878.2).
	孝昭皇帝	Xiào Zhāo Huángdì	(Emperor, 86–74 B.C.) This is his full posthumous name; it is most often abbreviated Zhāo-dì 昭帝.
	壹	*yī*	. . . ; all (GHY, citing this passage).
	決	*jué*	. . . ; decide (JM).

After line 16

16.2	堪	*kān*	Be able to; . . . (JM).
	委	*wěi*	. . .; entrust to; deliver to (GSR 357a).
	任	*rén* *rèn*	Anc. *ńźi̯əm*, to carry; Anc. *ńźi̯əm:*, burden (GSR 667f).
	壬	*rén*	Anc. *ńźi̯əm* (GSR 667a).
	之	*zhī*	Anc. *tśi* (GSR 962a).
	欲	*yù*	Anc. *i̯wok* (GSR 1202d).
	屬	*shǔ* *zhǔ*	Anc. *źi̯wok* be attached to; Anc. *tśi̯wok* to attach (GSR 1224s). → line 11.
16.3	署	*shǔ*	Office; . . . (JM).
	職任	*zhírèn*	Duties (M 9: 9586).
	親近	*qīnjìn*	Intimate and close (CY 2857.1).
	百物	*bǎiwù*	All kinds of things (M 8: 8197). (In the examples given by M the "things" are usually the products of craftsmen.)
16.5	曉	*xiǎo*	To know; . . . (JM).
16.6	拜	*bài*	→ line 15.
	拜職	*bàizhí*	Appoint to an official position (HY 6: 434).

Wáng Xiānqiān (p. 2a, line 2) gives several text examples which indicate with some certainty that *nèi* 內 in this sort of context means *shì* 室, "room".

17	先是	*xiānshì*	Before this (conventional phrase introducing a digression in a narrative) (CY 278.2).
	後元	Hòuyuán	→ line 12.
	侍中僕射	*shìzhōng* *púyè*	Supervisor of Palace Attendants (B). (B and JM transcribe 射 as *yè* rather than *shè*, but see CY 259.1, 870.3, GHY p. 216).

	莽	*mǎng*	. . . ; surname (CY 2657.1). Watson's reference (*Courtier and commoner*, p. 123, fn. 2) is to Dubs, vol. 2, p. 118, fn. 38.4.
	重合	Chónghé	Hàn prefecture west of modern Lèlíng 樂陵 County, Shāndōng (M 11: 418.1).
	逆	*nì*	To meet, join; to accept, receive; beforehand; contrariwise; to violate, go against; to anticipate, foresee; to rebel (JM).
	誅	*zhū*	To punish; to kill; to request, demand (GHY).
18	錄	*lù*	. . . to accept; to appoint (JM).
	封	*fēng*	To enfief; to seal (GHY).
	璽書	*xǐshū*	(Pre-Qin:) a letter sealed with an official seal; (Qin and after:) an Imperial decree (JM).
	發書	*fāshū*	. . . ; to open (a letter) (JM).
	從事	*cóngshì*	Administer affairs (CY 1081.3).
	遺詔	*yízhào*	→ line 15.
	秺	Dù	. . . place in modern Chéngwǔ County 成武縣, Shāndōng (CY 2304.3).
	安陽	Ānyáng	Hàn prefecture, modern Ānyáng Municipality, Hénán (CY 806.1).
19	博陸	Bólù	Han place name (CY 429.1, referring only to this passage). Later, in the Jìn period, the Hàn prefectures Bólíng 博陵 and Lùchéng 陸成 were combined to form Bólù, south of modern Lǐxiàn 蠡縣, Hébĕi (CY).
	捕	*bǔ*	To arrest (a criminal); to catch (fish) (JM).
	衛尉	*wèiwèi*	Commandant of the Guards (B).

Note that the Wáng Mǎng 王莽 mentioned here has no connection whatever with the man of exactly the same name who usurped the Hàn throne in A.D. 8.

	子男	*zǐnán*	Son (CY 774.1).

	侍中	*shìzhōng*	→ line 7.
	揚	*yáng*	To raise; praise; propagate; display; carry on; exert oneself; . . . (GHY).
	揚語	*yángyǔ*	\CY \M
	揚言	*yángyán*	To boast; to spread false propaganda (CY 1291.1).
20	群兒	*qún'ér*	Many children; a crowd of children (M 9: 71). (Here perhaps: "the old boys").
	切	*qiē*	. . . ; near;
		qiè	. . . ; earnest, sincere; urgent (GHY).
	讓	*ràng*	To reproach; to decline, refuse (GHY).
	切讓	*qièràng*	To reproach severely (HY 564.1).
	酖	*dān*	To be addicted to drink;
		zhèn	Poisonous wine; to poison with poisonous wine (CY 3132.2).

After line 20

20.1	莫	*mù*	Anc. *muo-*, evening, late.
		mò	Anc. *mâk*, not, not have.
		mò	Anc. *mɒk*, calm and respectful. (GSR 802a).
	戶	*hù*	Anc. *γuo:* (GSR 53a).
	莽	*mǎng*	Anc. *mwâng:*, grass, weeds (GSR 709a).

Ancient *muo:* should give modern Běijīng *mù* (Karlgren, *Compendium*, p. 325).

20.2	文穎	Wén Yǐng	According to Yán Shīgǔ's preface he was from Nányáng 南陽 and flourished at the end of the Hàn and the beginning of the Wèi 魏 period.
	嘉名	*jiāmíng*	Elegant name (CY 543.2).
	食邑	*shíyì*	To live on taxes from one's fief; a fief (HY 12: 482.2).

	北海[郡]	Běihǎi [jùn]	Han commandery, in modern Shāndōng (CY 390.3).
	河間[國]	Héjiān [guó]	A Hàn marquisate, in modern Héjiān County, Héběi (CY 1755.1).
	東郡	Dōngjùn	Han commandery, south of modern Púyáng County 濮陽縣, Hénán (CY 1527.2).

NB: See p. 2968 and Wáng Xiānqiān p. 2a, lines 7–10 for explanation of the editors' emendations. All versions have 北海河東城, but the fief is listed in *juàn* 18, p. 691, as 北海河間東郡. Yán Shīgǔ comments there that the original fief consisted of 北海 and 河間, while 東郡 was added later.

	鄉	*xiāng*	District (B). → line 1.
	聚	*jù*	Agglomeration (B). → line 1.
	公孫弘	Gōngsūn Hóng	(His biography in the *Shǐ jì* is translated by Watson, 2: 219–225.)
	平津鄉	Píngjīn xiāng	Han district, south of modern Yǎnshān County 鹽山縣, Héběi (M 4: 498.3).
20.3	右將軍	*yòu jiāngjūn*	General of the Right (B).
20.4	宣唱	*xuānchàng*	\HY
	宣	*xuān*	Spread, diffuse; proclaim, display; boastful; . . . (GSR 164t).
	唱	*chàng*	Take the lead (GSR 724d). Lead a chorus; sing; shout (JM).
20.6	深	*shēn*	Deep; extremely (GHY).
	責	*zé*	Demand; ask about; reproach, blame; duty;
		zhài	. . . (GHY).
21	沈靜	*chénjìng*	Self-possessed and tranquil (M 6: 971).
	詳審	*xiángshěn*	Composed and serious (only example is this passage); cautious and circumspect (HY 11: 207).
	詳	*xiáng*	In detail; precise, careful; exhaustive; cautious (GHY).

	審	*shěn*	In detail; precise, careful; to understand; to investigate (GHY).
	財	*cái*	. . . ; = 纔, only (GHY).
	尺	*chǐ*	In the Hàn period, ca. 23 cm; see *Dù liáng héng*, plates 4–28.
	寸	*cùn*	$\frac{1}{10}$ *chǐ* (GHY).
	皙	*xī*	White face; a variety of date (CY 2181.3). White (GSR 857d).
	白皙	*báixī*	Pure white skin (CY 2160.1).
	疏	*shū*	To dredge; to divide; to drift apart; sparse; coarse;
		shù	. . . ; memorial to the Emperor (GHY).
	眉目	*méimù*	Eyebrows and eyes; general appearance; . . . (CY 2204.2).
	須	*xū*	. . . ; = 鬚, mustache and beard (GHY). → line 42.
	䫇	*rán*	Side-whiskers (GHY, p. 275, under *xū* 須). = 髯.
	鬚髯	*xūrán*	Whiskers (HY 12: 754).
22	郎僕射	*lángpúyè*	Supervisor of the Gentlemen (B).
	竊	*qiè*	To steal; stealthily; secretly; privately; without permission (GHY).
	識	*shí*	To know; knowledge;
		zhì	To remember; to learn by heart; a mark (GHY).
	視	*shì*	To look; . . . (GHY).
	失	*shī*	. . . ; to err by (a certain amount) (this meaning is commonly seen in early Chinese mathematical texts, but is not found in GHY, CY, M, or HY).
	資性	*zīxìng*	Character, nature (CY 2960.3).
	端正	*duānzhèng*	Honest, upright, fair-minded; neat and tidy in appearance (CY 2342.3).

As Wáng Xiānqiān notes (p. 2b, lines 6–8), the passage which follows is quoted, with slight change, in *Zīzhì tōngjiàn* 資治通鑑 (Zhōnghuá Shūjú ed., Beijing 1956), *juàn* 22, p. 748.

	輔	*fŭ*	→ line 11.
	幼主	*yòuzhŭ*	An infant ruler (M 4: 530).
23	想聞	*xiăngwén*	Listen to with love and respect (M 4: 1102, referring only to this passage).
	風采	*fēngcăi*	Demeanour; (facial) expression; customs (CY 3406.1).
	一	*yī*	. . . ; entire (CY 1.1).
	驚	*jīng*	. . . ; startle, panic (GHY).
	召	*zhào*	Call, beckon (GHY). (GHY has *zhāo*, probably a typographical error).
	尚符璽郎 [中]	*shàng fúxĭ láng [zhōng]*	Gentleman-of-the-Palace Who is Master of Insignia and Imperial Seals (B).
24	按	*àn*	. . . ; to grasp (GHY).
	誼	*yì*	= 義 proper morals, behaviour, or principles; meaning; friendship (GHY).
	明	*míng*	. . . ; 次、下一個 next (GHY).
	詔	*zhào*	. . . ; decree of the Emperor (GHY).
	秩	*zhì*	Official rank; . . . (GHY).
	眾庶	*zhòngshù*	The common people; . . . (M 8: 220.1).
	多	*duō*	Many; to praise; only, merely (GHY).

After line 25

25.1	纔	*cái*	. . . ; only merely (GHY).
25.2	潔	*jié*	Clean; completely; pure (GHY).
	潔白	*jiébái*	A pure white colour (HY 6: 116.2).

	頰	*jiá*	Cheeks (GHY).
	晳	*xī*	Anc. *siek* (GSR 857d).
	先	*xiān*	Anc. *sien* (GSR 478a).
	歷	*lì*	Anc. *liek* (GSR 858e).
	髥	*rán* *ràn*	Anc. *ńźi̯äm;* Anc. *ńźi̯äm-* (GSR 622j, k: alternate pronunciations with same meaning).
	人	*rén*	Anc. *ńźi̯ĕn* (GSR 388a).
	占	*zhān*	Anc.*tśi̯äm* (GSR 618a).
25.3	識	*shí* *zhì*	Anc. *śi̯ək*, to know Anc. *tśi-*, to remember, record (GSR 920k).
	式	*shì*	Anc. *śi̯ək* (GSR 918f).
	志	*zhì*	Anc. *tśi-* (GSR 962e).
25.5	文采	*wéncǎi*	Rich and bright colours; literary or artistic talent (CY 1358.3).
25.6	變	*biàn*	. . . ; calamity, abnormal phenomenon (GHY).
	變難	*biànnàn*	Turmoil, social upheaval (HY 5: 536.1).
	收取	*shōuqǔ*	Take in care; confiscate, recapture (HY 5: 384.1).
26	左將軍	*zuǒ jiāngjūn*	→ line 15.
	結婚	*jiéhūn*	(Of families:) to become related by marriage; also, to become man and wife (CY 2425.2).
	親	*qīn*	Parents; closely related, close family; close to; to love; 親自 himself, herself; . . .
		qìn	In-laws (CY 2857.3).
	妻	*qī*	Wife;
		qì	To give a woman in marriage (GHY).
	姊	*zǐ*	→ line 3.

	因	*yīn*	. . . ; thereupon; to rely on; to take advantage of (GHY).

A useful diagram of these family relations is given in *Cambridge history*, pp. 182–183.

	[公]主	*[gōng]zhǔ*	Princess (B).
27	內	*nèi*	. . . ;
		nà	= 納 to insert, introduce; to admit, accept (GHY).
	後宮	*hòugōng*	Women's quarters in the palace (CY 1073.1).
	倢伃	*jiéyú*	→ line 11.
	票騎將軍	*piàojì jiāngjūn*	→ line 1.
	桑樂	Sānglè	\CY \DM \M
	休	*xiū*	To rest; . . . (GHY).
	沐	*mù*	To wash the head (GHY).
	休沐	*xiūmù*	(Of an official:) to rest and bathe, i.e. to take a holiday (CY 176.3).

Wáng Xiānqiān (p. 3a, line 2) notes a source which indicates that a Hàn official's "bath and hair-washing day" was every fifth day.

	輒	*zhé*	總是 altogether ; immediately; without authorization; 立即、就, immediately; to usurp authority (GHY).
	輒入	*zhérù*	To enter without authority; to enter freely (HY 9: 1253.1).
28	決事	*juéshì*	To decide matters (M 6: 955.2).
	尊盛	*zūnshèng*	Having high position and being influential and prosperous (M 4: 33.4).
	德	*dé*	. . . ; to feel grateful to (GHY).

	長公主	*zhǎng gōng-zhǔ*	Emperor's sisters, both older and younger (CY 3224.1, 3229.1). Senior Princess (B).
	內行	*nèixíng*	. . . ; concealed matters (CY 287.2). Activities inside one's home (M 1: 1044).
	修	*xiū*	. . . ; excellent, correct (GHY).
	近幸	*jìnxìng*	寵信 be specially fond of and trust unduly (a subordinate); a favourite of a ruler (CY 3048.1).
	河間	Héjiān	→ no. 2 after line 20.
	外人	*wàirén*	Other people; an outsider (CY 649.3). . . . ; paramour, secret lover (M 3: 330.4, referring to this passage only).
29	幸	*xìng*	. . . ; to hope to (GHY).
	尚	*shàng*	. . . ; to marry a female relative of the Emperor (GSR).
	國家	*guójiā*	. . . ; the state, the court (HY 3: 640.1).
	故事	*gùshì*	. . . ; precedent (HY 5: 432.1).
	令	*lìng*	To command; 使 to cause; if; . . . (GHY).
	光祿大夫	*guānglù dà-fū*	→ line 8.
	召見	*zhàojiàn*	To command a person to appear; to grant an audience to (CY 467.2).
30	長主	*zhǎngzhǔ*	= *zhǎnggōngzhǔ* 長公主, → line 28.
	數	*shù, cù, shǔ*	. . . ;
		shuò	Repeatedly (GHY).
	慙	*cán*	= 慚 ashamed, embarassed (CY 1161.1).
	九卿	*jiǔqīng*	The Nine Ministers (B).

Wáng Xiānqiān (p. 3a, lines 7–8) explains the ranks which the two men held.

31	椒房	Jiāofáng	Palace of the Empress (CY 1595.1).

中宮	*zhōnggōng*	Domicile of Empress; Empress (CY 86.3).
親	*qīn, qìn*	→ line 26.

皇后親安女 seems at first glance to mean, "The Empress was close to [Shàngguān] Ān's daughter". Clearly something is wrong here, since the Empress *was* Shàngguān Ān's daughter. Probably *qīn* 親 should be taken to mean "herself": A woman of the Shàngguān family herself had this high post, and Huò Guāng was merely her maternal grandfather, but the Huò family had much more power and prestige than they did. Watson (*Courtier and commoner*, p. 126) has another solution: he emends "Empress" to "Emperor".

	外祖	*wàizǔ*	Maternal grandfather (CY651.3).
	顧	*gù*	Turn the head and look at; visit; show consideration for; (adverb:) nevertheless (GHY).
	專制	*zhuānzhì*	To act arbitrarily (CY 873.2).
32	繇	*yáo*	. . .
		yóu	= 由, from (GHY).

After line 32

32.1	晉灼	Jìn Zhuó	According to Yán Shīgǔ's preface he was a man of Hénán 河南, and held the rank of *shàngshūláng* 尚書郎 in the Jìn 晉 period.
	漢語	*Hàn yǔ*	Xún Shuǎng 荀爽 [A.D. 128–190] collected together stories of Han affairs which could serve as admonishments; he titled it *Hàn yǔ*. (*Hòu Hàn shū*, juàn 62, p. 2057).
	嫡	*dí*	Principal wife (JM).
	嫡妻	*díqī*	Principal wife (HY 4: 406.1).
	東閭	Dōnglǘ	A surname (CY 1529.2).
	夫人	*fūrén*	Wife of a nobleman; wife of an Emperor; . . .
		fúrén	. . . (CY 699.3).
	昭后	Zhāo-hòu	Empress of Zhāo-dì 昭帝, → line 16.
32.2	食邑	*shíyì*	→ no. 2 after line 20.

	蓋侯	Gě hóu	His name was Wáng Chōng 王充; he succeeded to the marquisate in 132 B.C. (*Hàn shū, juàn* 18, p. 685).
	尚	*shàng*	→ line 29.
32.3	懷	*huái*	. . . ; to feel (love, hatred, etc.); remember fondly; incline toward; appease (GHY).
	恩德	*ēndé*	Favour, benevolence (M 4: 1037.3).
33	燕王旦	Yān wáng Dàn	→ line 10.
	怨望	*yuànwàng*	Resentful, dissatisfied (CY 1115.1).
	昭帝	Zhāo dì	→ line 16.
	御史大夫	*yùshǐ dàfū*	→ line 15.
	榷	*què*	To monopolize (GHY); a single-log bridge; state monopoly; to discuss (CY 1614,3).
	酒榷	*jiǔquè*	Tax on alcohol (CY 3130.1); state monopoly on alcohol (CY 1614.3, under 榷酤).

On the Hàn state monopolies on salt, iron, and alcohol see e.g. *Cambridge History*, pp. 582–3, 602–5.

	興利	*xīnglì*	To increase profits greatly (M 9: 450.2–3).
	伐	*fá*	. . . ; to boast about (*Zhuāng zǐ* 莊子: 自伐者無功) (GHY).
34	子弟	*zǐdì*	Sons and younger brothers; posterity in general; sons and nephews; . . . (CY 773.3–4).
	怨恨	*yuànhèn*	To bear a grudge against, to resent (M 4: 1012.3).
	通謀	*tōngmóu*	To conspire, collude (M 11: 66.3).
	詐	*zhà*	To deceive, swindle; feign, simulate, pretend (GHY).
35	都	*dū*	. . . ; to accumulate (of water); to occupy; beautiful; all, entirely; = *yú* 於; surname (CY 3108.3).
	肄	*yì*	To practise; to toil; to investigate; . . . (GHY).

都肄	*dūyì*	To inspect military manoeuvres (CY 3111.2, referring to this passage only).
郎	*láng*	→ line 7.
羽林	*yǔlín*	Name of a constellation; Emperor's private guard (CY 2502.3). Feathered Forest (B).
趩	*bì*	= 蹕, to clear the way when the Emperor is approaching (CY 3006.3).
稱蹕	*chēngbì*	\CY \M \HY
太官	*tàiguān*	Grand Provisioner (B).
引	*yǐn*	. . . ; 引用 to use (GHY). → line 56.
蘇武	Sū Wǔ	His biography, in *Hàn shū*, *juàn* 54, is translated in Watson, *Courtier and commoner*, pp. 34–45.
匈奴	Xiōngnú	An ethnic group of north China in ancient times (GHY). See *Cambridge History*, pp. 383–405.
拘留	*jūliú*	Detain, arrest (CY 1243.2).
36 降	*jiàng*	To fall; . . . ;
	xiáng	To surrender; to cause to surrender (GHY).
典屬國	*diǎn shǔguó*	Director of Dependent States (B).
大將軍	*dàjiāngjūn*	→ line 14.
長史	*zhǎngshǐ*	Chief Clerk (B).
敞	Chǎng	According to Yán Shīgǔ's comment his surname was Yáng 楊.
亡功	*wúgōng*	\CY \M \HY
無功	*wúgōng*	Having no accomplishments, no merit; . . . (M 7: 436.1–2). 亡 → line 41.
搜粟都尉	*sōusù dūwèi*	→ line 15.
擅	*shàn*	To monopolize; to propose unofficially; to possess; = 禪, to abdicate (GHY).

	調	*tiáo*	Harmony; to be in harmony; to adjust; . . .
		diào	. . . ; to transfer (to another post);
		zhōu	Morning (JM).
	莫府	*mùfǔ*	= 幕府, general's tent; general's office (CY 2658.2, 985.2). . . . ; general (HY 3: 754.1).
	校尉	*xiàowèi*	Colonel (B).
	專權	*zhuānquán*	To monopolize authority (CY 874.1).
37	自恣	*zìzì*	To indulge oneself, to be unrestrained (HY 8: 1342.2).
	非常	*fēicháng*	Not usual; sudden unforeseen event; not according to custom (CY 3359.3).
	符璽	*fúxǐ*	Official seal of a ruler (CY 2352.1).
	宿衛	*sùwèi*	To serve night guard duty; to guard, protect; . . . (HY 3: 1529.1).
	姦臣	*jiānchén*	Disloyal servant (CY 753.3).
	變	*biàn*	→ no. 6 after line 25.
	沐	*mù*	→ line 27.

As Wáng Xiānqiān notes (p. 3b, lines 1–3), there is another version of this letter in *Hàn shū*, *juàn* 63, pp. 2754–5. It is translated in Watson, *Courtier and commoner*, pp. 59–61.

	候司	*hòusì*	= 候伺, to investigate; to wait (HY 1: 1504).
	從中	*cóngzhōng*	In the middle; standing between two persons (M 4: 885).

Wáng Xiānqiān's comments (p. 3b, lines 22–23) indicate that he takes *cóngzhōng* 從中 to mean "from within the inner sanctum" (*jìnzhōng* 禁中) and *dāng* 當 to mean "on his own authority".

38	當與	*dāngyǔ*	\CY \M [Note *dǎngyǔ* 黨與 in line 44.]
	執退	*zhítuì*	\CY \M \HY

	執	*zhí*	To arrest; hold; take; preserve; grasp; be in charge of; . . . (JM).
	退	*tuì*	To retreat; repulse; depart; return; cancel, revoke; remove (JM).

After line 38

38.1	矜	*jīn*	To sympathize with; attach importance to; arrogant; to boast about (example 矜其功).
		qín	. . .
		guān	. . . (GHY).
38.2	孟康	Mèng Kāng	According to Yán Shīgǔ's preface he flourished in the Wèi period.
	總閱	*zǒngyuè*	\HY
	閱	*yuè*	Review (troops); examine; . . . (JM).
38.3	具	*jù*	To prepare food and drink; food and drink; to prepare; complete, perfect; completely; to declare, state; apparatus; ability; measure word (GHY).
38.5	調	*tiáo* *zhòu*	Anc. *d'ieu*, tune, adjust; . . . Anc. *ȶi̯əu-*, morning (GSR 1083x).
	選	*xuǎn*	Choose; elect; . . . (JM).
	徒	*tú*	Anc. *d'uo* (GSR 62e).
	釣	*diào*	Anc. *tieu-* (GSR 1120k).

Ancient *d'ieu-* should give modern Běijīng *diào* (Karlgren, *Compendium*, p. 345).

38.6	下	*xià*	Anc. *γa:*, down; Anc. *γa-*, descend (GSR 35a).
	胡	*hú*	Anc. *γuo* (GSR 49a′).
	稼	*jià*	Anc. *ka-* (GSR 32f).

	有司	*yǒusī*	Officials (CY 1476.1). M 5:1028 gives several usage examples, most of which concern officials whose duties have to do with punishment.
39	畫室	*huàshì*	House of Paintings (B).

Wáng Xiānqiān (p. 3b, line 12 – p. 4a, line 6) gives a long discussion of the opinions of various scholars through the ages on the meaning of *huàshì* 畫室.

	室	*shì*	房屋, house, building (GHY).
40	告罪	*gàozuì*	Lodge an accusation; announce an indictment; confess (HY 3: 215).
	詔	*zhào*	→ line 24.
	召	*zhào*	→ line 23.
	免	*miǎn*	To avoid; to remove; to discharge from office; to give birth; . . . (GHY).
	冠	*guān*	A cap;
		guàn	To wear a cap; ceremony of a boy's coming of age; . . . (GHY).
	免冠	*miǎnguān*	To remove the cap, signifying an apology for an offense (CY 281.2).
	頓首	*dùnshǒu*	→ line 13.
	詐	*zhà*	→ line 34.
41	亡	*wáng*	Flee, go into exile; absent; to lose; to die;
		wàng	= 忘 to forget;
		wú	= 無 not to have; not (GHY).
	亡罪	*wúzuì*	= 無罪 innocent; innocent person (M 1: 530).
	陛	*bì*	Staircase; palace staircase (GHY).
	陛下	*bìxià*	You, term of address to emperor (GHY).

Wáng Xiānqiān (p. 4a, line 10) says Guǎngmíng 廣明 was east of Cháng'ān, outside the Dōngdū Gate 東都門.

	都郎	*dūláng*	\B \CY \M \HY
	都	*dū*	→ line 35.
	屬耳	*shǔěr*	To eavesdrop; to listen attentively (CY 916.1).

Wáng Xiānqiān (p. 4a, line 10) says that in this sentence *ěr* 耳 is a final particle.

	調	*diào, tiáo, zhōu*	→ line 36.
42	須	*xū*	. . . ; to need (GHY).
	尚書	*shàngshū*	Master of Writing (B).
	果	*guǒ*	In the end; in fact; result; as a result; . . . (GHY).
	亡	*wáng, wàng, wú*	→ line 41.
43	懼	*jù*	To be afraid; to worry (GHY).
	遂	*suì*	. . . ; to exhaust, get to the bottom of (CY 3076.1, referring to this passage). → line 47.

After line 43

43.1	如淳	Rú Chún	According to Yán Shīgǔ's preface he was a man of Wèi 魏 in the Three Kingdoms 三國 period.
	近臣	*jìnchén*	Officials close to a ruler (CY 3047.3).
	計畫	*jìhuà*	To think, plan (CY 2874.2).
	彫畫	*diāohuà*	Carved and painted (HY 3: 1127).
43.2	著	*zhù*	To appear; apparent; be widely known as; to display; precedence; to write; writings; . . .
		zhuó	To wear, put on; to add, append, augmnent, apply (GHY, HY 9: 430).

43.3	亭	*tíng*	Commune; Officials' Hostel (B). → line 1.
	近耳	*jìn'ěr*	\CY \M
	屬、之、欲	*shǔ/zhǔ, zhī, yù*	→ no. 2 after line 16.
43.4	文穎	Wén Yǐng	→ no. 2 after line 20.
43.5	竟	*jìng*	To finish; finally; completely; result; investigate; . . . (GHY).
	窮竟	*qióngjìng*	Thoroughly investigate; research deeply; use up (HY 8: 468).
44	黨與	*dǎngyǔ*	同黨的人, henchmen (CY 3584.3).
	譖	*zèn*	To speak ill of, to slander (GHY).
	輒	*zhé*	→ line 27.
	忠臣	*zhōngchén*	A devoted servant (M 4: 971.3).
	屬	*shǔ, zhǔ*	→ line 11.
	輔	*fǔ*	→ line 11.
	毀	*huǐ*	To ruin; to slander (GHY).
	坐	*zuò*	. . . ; to face a judge in a legal proceeding (GHY).
45	伏兵	*fúbīng*	Troops waiting in ambush (CY 179.3). 伏 → line 72.
	格	*gé*	. . . ; to strike (GHY).
	格殺	*géshā*	擊殺, to kill in fighting. 相拒而殺曰格 (CY 1567.2).
	因	*yīn*	→ line 26.
	迎立	*yínglì*	To call someone to the throne (M 11: 5).
46	發覺	*fājué*	To expose, bring to light, discover (CY 2154.2).
	誅	*zhū*	→ line 17.
	宗族	*zōngzú*	Relatives on father's side (CY 814.3).

	自殺	*zìshā*	To commit suicide (CY2584.2).
	威	*wēi*	Power, prestige; to fear; to cause to fear (GHY).
	震	*zhèn*	To shake: . . . (GHY).
	冠	*guān, guàn*	→ line 40.
47	遂	*suì*	As a result; then, thereupon; unexpectedly (WYXC).
	委任	*wěirèn*	To entrust to (GHY).
	訖	*qì*	The end; to complete; until; to reach (GHY).
	充實	*chōngshí*	To increase; satisfied (CY 275.1).
	賓服	*bīnfú*	To pay homage to the Emperor (CY 2963.3).

After line 47

47.1	委、屬、之、欲	*wěi, shǔ/ zhǔ, zhī, yù*	→ no. 2 after line 16.
48	元平	Yuánpíng	Reign period, 74 B.C. (only one year).
	亡	*wáng, wàng, wú*	→ line 41.
	持	*chí*	. . . ; to help, support (GHY).
	本	*běn*	. . . ; 本來 originally, in essence, in fact (GHY).
49	失道	*shīdào*	To lose one's way; wicked, evil (CY 712.2).
	自安	*zìān*	Feel at ease; . . . (HY 8: 1312).
	舍	*shě*	. . . ; renounce, reject;
		shè	. . . (GHY).
50	可以	*kě yǐ*	(Not a binome in Classical Chinese).
	承	*chéng*	Carry in both hands; to receive (a command from a superior); inherit; continue; = 乘, to ride , take advantage of (GHY).

51	[楊]敞	[Yáng] Chǎng	→ line 36.
	丞相	*chéngxiàng*	Chancellor (B).
	擢	*zhuó*	To promote (GHY).
	九江	Jiǔjiāng	. . . ; a Hàn commandery, modern Jiǔjiāng Municipality, Jiāngxī (CY 103.1).
	太守	*tàishǒu*	→ line 4.
	即日	*jírì*	當天, same day; 不日, within a few days (CY 437.3).
	承	*chéng*	→ line 50.
	皇太后	Huáng Tài-hòu	Empress Dowager (B).
	詔	*zhào*	→ line 24.
	大鴻臚	*dà hónglú*	Grand Herald (B).
	少府	*shàofǔ*	Privy Treasurer (B).
	宗正	*zōngzhèng*	Director of the Imperial Clan (B).
52	光祿大夫	*guānglù dàfū*	→ line 8.
	中郎	*zhōngláng*	Gentleman-of-the-Household (B).
	中郎將	*zhōngláng jiàng*	\B Leader of Court Gentlemen (Hucker).
	迎	*yíng*	→ line 45
	昌邑	Chāngyì	Place in modern Jīnxiāng 金鄉 County, Shāndōng (CY 1406.2).
53	即位	*jíwèi*	To take the throne; to take one's seat (CY 437.3).
	淫亂	*yínluàn*	Deviant and debauched (M 7: 34).
	憂懣	*yōumèn*	Gloomy, depressed (CY 1163.1).
	獨	*dú*	Alone; lonely; 僅、只有 only (GHY).

	故吏	*gùlì*	A former official; a former subordinate (HY 5: 430).
	大司農	*dà sīnóng*	Grand Minister of Agriculture (B).
54	柱石	*zhùshí*	A person who assumes great responsibilities for the State (CY 1545.3).
	建白	*jiànbái*	State one's views (CY 1031.3, referring to this passage only).
	[皇]太后	*[Huáng] Tàihòu*	→ line 51.
	更	*gēng*	To change; alternately; to undergo, experience; . . .
		gèng	Even more; again; . . . (JM).
	選賢	*xuǎnxián*	To appoint a person of ability (HY 10: 1244).
55	伊尹	Yī Yǐn	A high official of Tāng 湯, the first king of Shāng (CY 181.3 has a brief resumé of his story).
	相	*xiāng*	. . .
		xiàng	. . . ; to assist; the highest official of a ruler (GHY).
	太甲	Tài Jiǎ	A grandson of Tāng 湯 (CY 701.3 has a brief resumé of his story).
	宗廟	*zōngmiào*	Place where an Emperor or aristocrat sacrificed to his ancestors (CY 815.2).
56	引	*yǐn*	. . . ; 召引 to summon (GHY). → line 35.
	給事中	*jǐshìzhōng*	Serving Within the Palace (B). *Jǐshì* → line 1.
	圖計	*túji*	To plan, arrange; a plan, a strategem (HY 3: 666.2).
57	遂	*suì*	→ line 47.
	丞相	*chéngxiàng*	→ line 51.
	御史	*yùshǐ*	Secretary (B).
	列侯	*lièhóu*	Full Marquis (B). 侯 → line 12.

中二千石	*zhòng èr-qiān shí*	Official Ranking Fully 2000 Shí (B). [Cf. line 93.]
大夫	*dàfū*	Grandee (B).
博士	*bóshì*	Erudit (B).
會議	*huìyì*	To assemble and discuss a matter (CY 1471.1).
未央宮	Wèiyāng Gōng	Eternal Palace (normal residence of Emperor) (B).
昏亂	*hūnluàn*	Black-hearted and disorderly (M 5: 786).
58 社稷	*shèjì*	→ line 11.
如何	*rúhé*	怎樣 how? 奈何 what is to be done? . . . (CY 736.1).
驚鄂	*jīng'è*	= 驚愕, extremely shocked and amazed (HY 12: 890, 891). *è* 愕 → no. 7 after line 63.
失色	*shīsè*	To have a frivolous facial expression; to change facial expression in shock (CY 711.1).
發言	*fāyán*	To state one's opinion; a stated opinion; to express in words; open one's mouth to speak; to threaten (HY 8: 549).
唯唯	*wěiwěi*	Yes (expressing respect and obedience); yes (expressing acquiescence without indicating whether the thing requested is possible); acquiescent (CY 528.2). wěi 唯 → line 62.
前	*qián*	. . . ; to go forward (GHY).
59 幼孤	*yòugū*	A young orphan (HY 4: 430).
寄	*jì*	. . . ; entrust to the care of (GHY).
群下	*qúnxià*	Many inferiors; many disciples; many subjects (M 9: 69).
鼎沸	*dǐngfèi*	Seething like a cauldron (CY 3589.3).
傾	*qīng*	Tilt; collapse; . . . (GHY).

60 謚 *shì* Posthumous name of a ruler; . . . (GHY).

The full posthumous names of all the Hàn Emperors begin with the character *xiào* 孝, but these names were and are commonly abbreviated, so that for example Xiào Wǔ Huángdì 孝武皇帝, "The Filial and Martial Emperor", is referred to as Wǔ dì 武帝.

長 *cháng* . . . ; 長久 for a long time;

zhǎng . . . ; to foster, to nurture (CY 3223.1).

以長有天下 may mean "because they possessed the Empire for a long time [*cháng* 長]" or "because they possessed and nurtured [*zhǎng* 長] the Empire".

血食 *xuèshí* Blood sacrifice (CY 2797.2).

絕祀 *juésì* To break off the sacrifices; metaphor for the destruction of a state (CY 2430.2).

令 *lìng* → line 29.

面目 *miànmù* Face, appearance; "face", reputation (CY 3362.1).

61 地下 *dìxià* 黃泉, realm of the dead (M 3: 130, citing example from *Hàn shū*, biography of 王陵: 何面目見高帝於地下乎).

得 *dé* . . . ; to be possible (GHY).

旋踵 *xuánzhǒng* Turn on one's heel, disappear in a hurry; shrink back, flinch (CY 1392.2).

後應 *hòuyìng* To respond afterward (M 4: 830, citing post-Hàn examples only).

斬 *zhǎn* Kill; decapitate (GHY).

九卿 *jiǔqīng* → line 30.

責 *zé, zhài* → no. 6 after line 20.

62 匈匈 *xiōngxiōng* Sound of fighting or disorder (GHY).

受難 *shòunàn* To be blamed (HY 2: 888).

唯 *wěi* . . . ; sentence prefix indicating hope (GHY).

After line 63

63.1	満	*mǎn*	Anc. *muân*: (GSR 183c).
	懣	*mǎn* *mèn*	Anc. *muân:*, grieved; Anc. *muən:*, *muən-*, grieved (GSR 183g).
	悶	*mèn* *mén*	Anc. *muən-*, sad, dull, stupid; Anc. *muən*, unconsciously (GSR 441d).
63.2	梁	*liáng*	Bridge; roof beam (GHY).
	承	*chéng*	→ line 50.
	礎	*chǔ*	Stone at base of column (GHY).
63.3	立議	*lìyì*	\CY \M \HY
	議	*yì*	To discuss; to criticize; a proposal; . . . (GHY).
	白	*bái*	. . . ; (inferior to superior:) to inform, to explain (GHY).
63.4	涉學	*shèxué*	To study, acquire learning (HY 5: 1199.2).
63.5	商書	*Shāng shū*	The 17 chapters of the *Shū jīng* 書經 which concern the Shāng dynasty (M 2: 1053.3).
	太甲	*Tàijiǎ*	One of the forged chapters of the *Book of documents*; . . . (M 3:524.3). → line 55. Translated in Legge, *Shoo king*, pp. 199–212.
63.7	阻礙	*zǔài*	To obstruct and separate (M 11:796).
	依順	*yīshùn*	To be obedient to; to submit to (HY 1: 1352.1).
	鄂	*è*	Ancient place name; used for 愕、諤、蕚、堮.
	愕	*è*	Amazed; = 諤 honest in speech (GHY).
63.9	速決	*sùjué*	To make a decision quickly (M 11: 70.4).
63.10	憂責	*yōuzé*	To assume responsibility; duty, heavy responsibility (HY 7: 688.2).
63.11	一	*yī*	→ line 23.
64	群臣	*qúnchén*	Subjects, retainers, vassals (M 9: 71.4). 羣 = 群.

俱	*jù*	Together; all (GHY).
見白	*jiànbái*	\CY \M
具陳	*jùchén*	To explain fully (HY 2: 110.1).
具	*jù*	→ no. 3 after line 38.
陳	*chén*	To display; to state; . . .
	zhèn	. . . (GHY).
狀	*zhuàng*	. . . ; situation, state of affairs (GHY).
陳狀	*chénzhuàng*	To describe the situation (M 11: 864.4).
駕	*jià*	To harness a horse to a cart; to drive (a vehicle); a vehicle; royal vehicle; royalty; transcend, surpass; framework (GHY).
車駕	*chējià*	Horse-carriage; metaphor for ruler (CY 3014.2).
幸	*xìng*	. . . ; to go to (special term used only of an Emperor) (GHY).
承明	Chéngmíng	A hall (*diàn* 殿) in the Wèiyāng Palace 未央宮 of the Hàn; . . . (CY 1228.1, 1229.3). Wèiyāng Palace → line 57.
65 禁門	*jìnmén*	Gates of Imperial palace (M 8: 482).
毋	*wú*	不要 don't; 無 not have; 不 not (GHY).
群臣	*qúnchén*	→ line 64.
內	*nèi, nà*	→ line 27.
輦	*niǎn*	Sedan chair; (from Qín onward:) the Emperor's conveyance (GHY).
溫室	*wēnshì*	A warm building; name of a hall (*diàn* 殿) in both the Chánglè Gōng 長樂宮 and the Wèiyāng Gōng 未央宮 of the Hàn (CY 1849.1).
中黃門	*zhōng-huángmén*	Palace Attendant of the Yellow Gates (which gave access to the Emperor's private quarters) (B).
宦	*huàn*	Servant; official; eunuch (GHY).

	扇	*shān*	Fan; to fan;
		shàn	Door leaf; fan (GHY).
	何為	*héwèi*	Why; of what use;
		héwéi	What are you doing? (M 1: 695.1).
66	跪	*guì*	→ line 5.
	徐	*xú*	Slowly (GHY).
	徐之	*xúzhī*	\CY \M \HY
67	何乃	*hénǎi*	何能, 怎麼能 (CY 187.3).
	驚人	*jīngrén*	To startle someone; to cause a sensation (M 12: 559.4).
	驅	*qū*	To ride a horse; to expel, drive out (GHY).
	驅出	*qūchū*	To expel, drive out (M 12: 549.3).
	金馬門	Jīnmǎ Mén	(CY 3165.3 tells the story of how this gate got its name).
	羽林騎	*yǔlínjì*	Cavalry of the Feathered Forest (B).
	收縛	*shōufù*	Arrest, round up, apprehend (M 5: 468).
68	廷尉	*tíngwèi*	Commandant of Justice (B).
	詔獄	*zhàoyù*	A prison; . . . (CY 2886.1).
	故	*gù*	. . . ; former; deceased (CY 1340.1, M 5: 491.4).
	侍中	*shìzhōng*	→ line 7.
	中臣	*zhōngchén*	. . . ; a eunuch (HY 1: 588.2).
	侍	*shì*	To accompany a superior; to wait upon, attend (GHY).
	侍守	*shìshǒu*	\CY \M \HY
	敕	*chì*	Warn, exhort; command of the Emperor (GHY).
	謹	*jǐn*	Careful (GHY).

	宿衛	*sùwèi*	→ line 37.
	卒	*zú*	Soldier; to die; finish; finally, in the end;
		cù	Suddenly (GHY).
	物故	*wùgù*	To die; . . . (CY 1984.3).
	裁	*cái*	To tailor; to cut off; . . . (GHY).
	自裁	*zìcái*	To commit suicide (GHY, p. 19).
69	負	*fù*	. . . ; 辜負 to let down, be unworthy of (CY 2948.1). → lines 12, 111.
	從官	*zòngguān*	(CY 1081.3) Attendant Official (B). (B has *cóngguān*).
	得罪	*dézuì*	Become guilty (CY 1079.3).
70	繫	*xì*	Restrain, arrest (GHY).
	頃之	*qǐngzhī*	不久 soon (GHY).
	詔	*zhào*	→ line 24.
	召	*zhào*	→ line 23.
	聞召	*wénzhào*	\CY \M
	意恐	*yìkǒng*	\CY \M \HY
	意	*yì*	. . . ; to suspect;
		yī	An exclamation (GHY).
	被	*bèi*	Clothing; passive marker;
		pī	To wear (GHY).
71	襦	*rú*	Short outer garment (GHY). (Hayashi, pp. 2, 9; fig. 1–17).
	盛服	*shèngfú*	Neatly dressed (CY 2188.1).
	武帳	*wǔzhàng*	Canopy in which weapons are placed, used by ruler (CY 1671.3).

	侍御	*shìyù*	An attendant (CY 204.3).
	期門	*qīmén*	Attendant at the Gates (B).
	持兵	*chíbīng*	Hold weapons in the hand; to be armed (HY 6: 549).
	武士	*wǔshì*	Soldier, warrior (CY 1669.3).
	陛戟	*bìjǐ*	Stand guard holding halberds beside the staircase (CY 3271.3, referring to this passage only). 陛 → line 41.
	陳列	*chénliè*	To arrange, spread out (M 11: 875.3).
72	伏前	*fúqián*	\CY \M \HY
	伏	*fú*	趴 to lie on one's stomach; to subdue; to submit to (a punishment); . . . (GHY).
	前	*qián*	→ line 58.
	聽詔	*tīngzhào*	\CY \M \HY
	連名	*liánmíng*	Joint signature (M 11: 86).
	尚書令	*shàngshū-lìng*	Prefect of the Masters of Writing (B).
	奏	*zòu*	To advance; to present; to address a ruler; a memorial to the throne; to play music (GHY).
	讀奏	*dúzòu*	To read a memorial aloud to the Emperor (M 10: 612.3).

After line 72

72.1	猝	*cù*	Suddenly (GHY).
72.3	如淳	Rú Chún	→ no. 1 after line 43.
	晉灼	Jìn Zhuó	→ no. 1 after line 32.
	革襦	*gérú*	\CY \M \HY

The long quotation which follows here (lines 73–107) is clearly an official document which Bān Gù copied into his text. My students and I find it much more difficult than the rest of the biography. The great number of comments which Yán Shīgǔ found it necessary to include, and the number of contradictory comments by others which he cites, indicate that ancient readers also found the passage difficult. Wáng Xiānqiān, on the other hand, gives very few comments, perhaps because he too had difficulty understanding it.

73	丞相	*chéngxiàng*	→ line 51.
	大司馬	*dàsīmǎ*	→ line 14.
	大將軍	*dàjiāngjūn*	→ line 14.
	車騎將軍	*chējì jiāngjūn*	→ line 14.
	度遼將軍	*dù Liáo jiāngjūn*	General Who Crosses the Liao River (B). 度 = 渡.
	前將軍	*qiánjiāngjūn*	General of the Van (B).
74	後將軍	*hòu jiāngjūn*	General of the Rear (B).
	御史大夫	*yùshǐ dàfū*	→ line 15.
	宜春	Yíchūn	Name of two different Hàn prefectures: (1) modern Yíchūn, County, Jiāngxī; (2) southeast of modern Rǔ'nán 汝南 County, Hénán.
	當塗	Dāngtú	A Hàn prefecture, modern Dāngtú, Ānhuī (CY 2124.3).
75	隨桃	Suítáo	\CY \M \DM
	杜	Dù	. . . ; ancient state; surname (CY 1513.2).
	屠耆	*túqí*	According to the *Shǐ jì*, a word in the Xiōngnú language meaning *xián* 賢, a wise person (CY 913.1).
	太僕	*tàipú*	→ line 15.
	太常	*tàicháng*	Grand Master of Ceremonies (B).
	大司農	*dà sīnóng*	→ line 53.
76	宗正	*zōngzhèng*	→ line 51.

	少府	*shàofŭ*	→ line 51.
	廷尉	*tíngwèi*	→ line 68.
	執金吾	*zhíjīnwú*	Bearer of the Gilded Mace (B).
	大鴻臚	*dà hónglú*	→ line 51.
77	左馮翊	*zuŏpíngyì*	Eastern Supporter (B). (翊 = 翌).
	右扶風	*yòufúfēng*	Western Sustainer (B).

From 104 B.C. the region of the capital was divided into three parts, which were administered by three officials:

jīngzhàoyĭn 京兆尹, Governor of the Capital
zuŏpíngyì 左馮翌, Eastern Supporter
yòufúfēng 右扶風, Western Sustainer

Together these were called the *sānfŭ* 三輔, Three Adjuncts (B, p. 87).

	長信[宮]	Chángxìn [gōng]	Palace of Prolonged Trust (B; CY 3226.2).
	少府	*shàofŭ*	→ line 51.
	典屬國	*diăn shŭguó*	→ line 36.
	京輔都尉	*jīngfŭ dūwèi*	Chief Commandant of the Adjunct Capital Region (B).
78	司隸校尉	*sīlì xiàowèi*	Colonel Director of the Retainers (B).
	諸吏	*zhūlì*	Inspector of Officials (B).
	文學	*wénxué*	Literary Scholar (B).
	光祿大夫	*guānglù dà-fū*	→ line 8.
79	太中大夫	*tàizhōng dà-fū*	Grand Palace Grandee (B).
	昧死	*mèisĭ*	Rashly risking death (polite formula in a memorial to a superior) (GHY).
80	頓首	*dùnshŏu*	→ line 13.

	死罪	*sǐzuì*	Guilty of a capital offense; a polite formula in memorials and letters ("risking death") (CY 1681.1).
	宗廟	*zōngmiào*	→ line 54.
	總壹	*zǒngyī*	= 總一 to unite (M 8: 1161.4, .3).
	慈	*cí*	Love (usually referring to parents' love for their children) (CY 1147.2).
	慈孝	*cíxiào*	To love one's parents and render filial piety (M 4: 1147.1).
	禮誼	*lǐyì*	The correct Way which men must tread (M 8: 503.4).
	誼	*yì*	→ line 24.
	賞罰	*shǎngfá*	Praise and blame, reward and punishment; . . . (M 10: 776.1).
81	孝昭皇帝	Xiào Zhāo Huángdì	→ line 16.
	棄	*qì*	To abandon (GHY).
	棄天下	*qì tiānxià*	To renounce the throne; euphemism for the death of an Emperor (HY 4: 1122).
	棄世	*qìshì*	. . . ; euphemism for death (CY 1585.2).
	議	*yì*	→ no. 3 after line 63.
	亡	*wáng, wàng, wú*	→ line 41.
	嗣	*sì*	→ line 11.
82	宗正	*zōngzhèng*	→ line 51.
	大鴻臚	*dà hónglú*	→ line 51.
	光祿大夫	*guānglù dàfū*	→ line 8.
	奉	*fèng*	→ line 8.

	節	*jié*	Staff of Authority, "consisting of a long piece of bamboo with a pendant at the top. It conferred on the messenger special powers which normally were a prerogative of the emperor" (B, p. 50).
	奉節	*fèngjié*	To hold the staff of authority, i.e. to be sent out on a mission (HY 2: 1513.1).
	使徵	*shǐzhēng*	\CY \M \HY
	徵	*zhēng*	. . . ; apointment, call to court (GHY).
	典	*diǎn*	. . . ; 主管 to take responsibility for (GHY).
	喪	*sāng*	Funeral; mourning;
		sàng	To lose, forfeit; to be defeated (JM).
	服	*fú*	Clothing; to wear; . . . (GHY).

Yán Shīgǔ states in note 32 that *diǎn sāngfú* 典喪服 means to be the chief mourner, but Wáng Xiānqiān (p. 7a, lines 8–9) argues that the sentence ends with *sāng*.

	斬縗	*zhǎncuī*	A specific type of funeral clothing (CY 532.1, under 喪服).
	悲哀	*bēiāi*	Grief and suffering (CY 1137.1).
	禮誼	*lǐyì*	→ line 80.
83	居	*jū*	To sit; to reside; residence; to stop, stay; to fix, regularise; to be at (a certain place); to serve as; . . .
		jī	Particle like *hū* 乎 or *qí* 其 (JM).
	素食	*sùshí*	To eat without working; to eat uncooked food; ordinary food; to eat vegetables and not meat (CY 2402.3).
	從官	*zòngguān*	→ line 69.
	略	*lüè*	Boundary; to make an inspection tour; to rob, plunder, seize; a scheme, strategem; roughly; approximate; a tiny amount (GHY).
	女子	*nǚzǐ*	Girl, woman, female (M 3: 616.2).

	載	*zài*	To load; to ride in; . . .
		zǎi	To record; year (JM).
	衣	*yī*	. . . ; a cover or sheath (CY 2811).
	衣車	*yīchē*	A carriage for clothing; a carriage with a screen (CY 2812.1).
	傳舍	*zhuànshè*	→ line 4.
	始	*shǐ*	. . . ; 剛才 just (WYXC).
	謁見	*yèjiàn*	To have audience with (a ruler) (M 10: 546.4).
	皇太子	Huáng Tàizǐ	Heir-apparent (B).
	常	*cháng*	永久 everlasting; 規律 regular; 常常 often; 平常 ordinary; = 嘗 already, aspect marker (GHY).
84	豚	*tún*	Small pig (GHY).
	信璽、行璽	*xìnxǐ, xíngxǐ*	[See Yán Shīgǔ's comment, note 34].
	大行	*dàxíng*	. . . ; to go and not return: euphemism for death of Emperor, also, the carrying of the Emperor's coffin to the tomb (CY 663.3). [The example cited by CY is consistent with the interpretation of *dàxíng* as "coffin", see note 34.]
	就次	*jiùcì*	To go to an inferior place (M 4: 118, with example from description of funeral ritual in *Yílǐ* 儀禮).
	次	*cì*	. . . ; temporary quarters (GHY).
	更	*gēng, gèng*	→ line 54.
	發	*fā*	. . . ; 打開 to open (GHY).
	封	*fēng*	→ line 18.
	節	*jié*	→ line 82.
	引內	*yǐnnà*	\CY \M \HY 內 → line 27.
	引納	*yǐnnà*	Draw in, pull in, lead in (M 4: 689).

85	騶	*zōu*	Groom; mounted attendant;
		qū	= 趨 to hasten (GHY).
	宰	*zǎi*	Butcher (B). Senior official of a district; (pre-Han:) Prime minister; domestic slave; to dominate; officiate at a sacrifice; butcher (GHY).
	官奴	*guānnú*	Government slaves (CY 821.1).
	常	*cháng*	→ line 83.
	與	*yǔ*	To give; to associate with; together with;
		yù	To participate; to praise; to help;
		yú	Final particle (GHY).
	居	*jū, jī*	→ line 83.
	禁闥	*jìntà*	→ line 8.
	敖戲	*áoxì*	嬉戲 to play, to sport (CY 1343.2).
	暮	*mù*	Evening; late (GHY).
	朝暮	*zhāomù*	早晚 morning and evening; 不久 soon (CY 1490.3).
86	臨	*lín*	To look down upon; to govern; to arrive; to face; . . . ;
		lìn	To weep (GHY).
	侍中	*shìzhōng*	→ line 7.
	問	*wèn*	. . . ; to extend greetings to (GHY).
	中御府	*zhōng yùfǔ*	Palace Wardrobe (B).
	令	*lìng*	→ line 29.
	奉	*fèng*	→ line 8.
	黃金	*huángjīn*	Gold; . . . (GHY).
87	斤	*jīn*	A kind of axe; a unit of weight (GHY). In the Hàn, ca. 250 g (DLH).

	妻	*qī, qì*	→ line 26.
	取	*qǔ*	. . . ; to acquire, gain, achieve; = 娶, to take a wife (GHY).
	前殿	*qiándiàn*	The principal hall in the palace (HY 2: 134.2).
	樂府	*yuèfǔ*	Bureau of Music (B).
	引內	*yǐnnà*	→ line 84.
	歌吹	*gēchuī*	Sound of singing and musical instruments (CY 1657.3).
	俳倡	*páichāng*	Acrobatics and music (CY 234.2).
88	會	*huì*	→ line 4.
	磬	*qìng*	An ancient percussion instrument, carved of fine stone or jade (JM).
	泰壹	Tàiyī	\CY \M
	泰一	Tàiyī	Name of a god of the heavens (CY 1745.2).
	輦道	*niǎndào*	A way inside a palace on which a sedan chair can be carried (CY 3026.2).
	牟首	Móushǒu	Place name (CY 1982.1, referring to this passage only).
	牟	*móu*	Sound made by a cow; to take; = 侔 equivalent (GHY).
	悉	*xī*	Detailed, thorough; to describe in detail; exhaustively; all, entire (GHY).
	奏	*zòu*	→ line 72.
	眾	*zhòng*	Many; ordinary people, everyone (GHY).
89	長安廚	Cháng'ān chú	The Kitchen of Cháng'ān (B).
	太牢	*tàiláo*	. . . ; sacrifice of an ox, a sheep, and a pig (CY 702.2).
	牢	*láo*	Pen where sacrificial animals are kept; sacrificial animals; prison (GHY).

	具	*jù*	→ no. 3 after line 38.
	祠	*cí*	To sacrifice; . . . (GHY).
	閣	*gé*	A raised wooden road; a bridge connecting two buildings; a type of small building; a storehouse for books and documents; an office; . . . (GHY).
	閣室	*géshì*	A side-chamber in a *gédào* 閣道 (only example is this passage); . . . (HY 12: 114).
	啗	*dàn*	To eat (GHY, referring to this passage); give to eat; . . . (GHY).
	駕	*jià*	→ line 64.
	法駕	*fǎjià*	Emperor's carriage (CY 1751.3).
	軒	*xuān*	Carriage of an aristocrat; floor; railing; . . . ; window; door; a carriage which is high in front and low in back; high; to hover in the air (GHY).
	皮軒	*píxuān*	Carriage made of tiger skin – the Han Emperors had carriages of this type (CY 2183.2).
	鸞	*luán*	A kind of bird in ancient myth; = 鑾, a kind of bell, often used on royal carriages (GHY).
	鸞旗	*luánqí*	A banner on the Emperor's carriage – it was red, plaited of feathers, with a *luán*-bird embroidered on it (CY 3551.2).
	驅馳	*qūchí*	Drive fast, chase (CY 3465.2).
	北宮	Běigōng	Northern Palace (B).
	桂宮	Guìgōng	\B
	桂	*guì*	木犀 sweet-scented osmanthus; 肉桂 Chinese cassia tree (CY 1559.3).
90	弄	*nòng*	To play with; to play games; to play a musical instrument; a popular song (GHY).
	彘	*zhì*	Pig (GHY).
	騎乘	*qíchéng*	To ride a horse; 騎 to ride a horse and 乘 to ride in a wagon (M 12: 531.3).

	遊戲	*yóuxì*	To romp and play (CY 3072.1).
	掖庭	*yètíng* (B: *yìtíng*)	Side-chambers in a palace where concubines live (CY 1268.3). Lateral Courts (harem) (B).
	宮人	*gōngrén*	Palace Maid: "government female slaves, aged eight years or more, who acted as attendants to the Empress and the harem ladies. . . . At thirty-five years of age they were dismissed to be married." (B).
91	淫亂	*yínluàn*	→ line 53.
	掖庭令	*yètínglìng*	Prefect of the Lateral Courts (B).
	泄	*xiè*	Flow out; express grievances; leak, divulge, reveal; . . . (GHY).
	泄言	*xièyán*	\CY \M \HY
	要斬	*yāozhǎn*	= 腰斬 to cut in two at the waist (M 10: 308, CY 2565.3).

After line 91

91.32	喪服	*sāngfú*	Funeral clothing; chapter of *Yí lǐ* 儀禮 (CY 532.1).
	喪主	*sāngzhǔ*	Chief mourner (CY 532.1).
	縗裳	*cuīcháng*	\CY \M
	縗	*cuī*	Ancient funeral clothing, made of hemp and open at the breast (GHY).
	裳	*cháng*	Ancient type of underwear (a type of shirt worn by both sexes) (GHY).
	緶	*biàn*	. . . ; hem (CY 2456.1).
	直	*zhí*	. . . ; 盡，只是 only (GHY).
	斬割	*zhǎngē*	\HY
	步	*bù*	Anc. *b'uo-* (GSR 73a).
	千	*qiān*	Anc. *ts'ien* (GSR 365a).

The *fǎnqiè* gloss seems to give a non-existent Ancient pronunciation.

91.33	菜食	*càishí*	To eat vegetarian food (HY 9: 446.2).
	肉食	*ròushí*	To hold a high position; to eat meat (HY 8: 1062.1).
	居喪	*jūsāng*	To be in the mourning period for an ancestor in the direct line of descent (CY 906.2).
	失	*shī*	→ line 22.
	喪服	*Sāngfú*	→ no. 32 after line 91.
	王莽傳	*Wáng Mǎng zhuàn*	The biography of Wáng Mǎng, *juàn* 99 of the *Hàn shū*. The place cited here is on p. 4050, with a comment by Yán Shīgǔ, no. 12 on p. 4051. See also Dubs, vol. 3, p. 153.
91.34	符節	*fújié*	Tallies; credentials; . . . (HY 8: 1125.1–2).
	符節臺	*fújié tái*	\HY
	符節令	*fújié lìng*	Prefect of Insignia and Credentials (B). 節 → line 84.
	臺	*tái*	A suffix in many agency names (Hucker).
	柩	*jiù*	Coffin (GHY).
91.35	國器	*guóqì*	Things needed by the state; the talent needed for governing; treasures of the state (HY 3: 646.1).
	緘	*jiān*	Twine, rope; to seal; . . . (GHY).
	緘封	*jiānfēng*	To seal (CY 2452.3).
	退還	*tuìhuán*	To return, turn back; to give back (HY 10: 844.2).
	次	*cì*	→ line 84.
	遂爾	*suìěr*	\CY \M
	遂	*suì*	→ line 47.
	爾	*ěr*	. . . ; suffix added to adjectives and adverbs (GHY).
	漏	*lòu*	To leak; to divulge; a water clock (GHY).

	發漏	*fālòu*	\CY \M
	發泄	*fāxiè*	To spread out, to diffuse (M 7: 1223.3). 泄 → line 91.
	發露	*fālù*	To expose; to be exposed (M 7: 1226.3).
	凡人	*fánrén*	Ordinary people; . . . (CY 332.2).
	重慎	*zhòngshèn*	Discreet, prudent, respectful (M 11: 423.3).
91.36	工	*gōng*	Anc. *kung* (GSR 1172a).
	衡	*héng*	Anc. *ɣɒng* (GSR 748h).
	更	*gēng*	Anc. *kɒng*, change;
		gèng	Anc. *kɒng-*, again, still more (GSR 745a).
	次	*cì*	. . . ; next (GHY).
91.37	署	*shǔ*	衙門 office; to inscribe; . . . (GHY).
	節	*jié*	→ line 82.
91.38	哭臨	*kūlìn*	Ceremonial wailing at the funeral of an Emperor (CY 519.3).
	力	*lì*	Anc. *li̯ək* (GSR 928a).
	禁	*jìn*	Anc. *ki̯əm-* (GSR 655k).
	臨	*lín*	Anc. *li̯əm*, approach . . . ;
		lìn	Anc. *li̯əm-*, ceremonial wailing (GSR 669e).
91.39	更互	*gēnghù*	Alternately, by turns (M 5: 963).
91.41	俳優	*páiyōu*	Musical entertainers (CY 234.2).
	諧戲	*xiéxì*	Romp and frolic (M 10: 527).

Should there be a comma in the first sentence of this comment?

91.42	柩	*jiù*	→ no. 34.
	冢	*zhǒng*	A large tomb; . . . (GHY).
	便	*biàn*	就 (GHY).

	胡、稼、下	*hú, jià, xià*	→ no. 6 after line 38.
91.43	鄭氏	Zhèng shì	(According to Yán Shīgǔ's introduction, p. 4, his name may have been Dé 德).
	觀	*guān*	. . . ; a view;
		guàn	High buildings on either side of an ancestor temple or the main gate of a palace; Daoist temple (GHY).
	閣道	*gédào*	. . . ; raised path between buildings; 棧道 plank road built along the face of a cliff (CY 3246.1).
	屏	*píng*	Screen; small wall facing a gate;
		bǐng	To remove; to hide (GHY).
	屏面	*píngmiàn*	Something to hide the face with (CY 902.2).
	隔	*gé*	To isolate (GHY).
	哀戚	*āiqī*	Grief (M 2: 999.4).
	上林苑	Shànglín Yuàn	Park of the Supreme Forest (in Cháng'ān) (B).
	衰	*shuāi*	Weak, declining;
		cuī	To reduce; to order by rank; = 縗, hemp mourning garment worn draped over the chest (GHY). → line 82, note 32 after line 91.
	絰	*dié*	A hemp mourning sash, worn at the waist or on the head (GHY).
	衰絰	*cuīdié*	Funeral clothing; to wear funeral clothing; to be in mourning (HY 9: 33.1).
	左思	Zuǒ Sī	A poet of the Western Jìn 西晉 period (CY 958.1–2).
	吳都賦	*Wú dū fù*	"Rapture on the capital of Wú", a poem by Zuǒ Sī. Translated in Knechtges, *Wen xuan 1*, pp. 373–428.
	劉逵	Liú Kuí	A man of the Jìn 晉 period, who wrote a book entitled *Sāngfú yàojì* 喪服要記 (M 2: 318.1).

	塗	*tú*	Mud; road; method; to paint or daub; . . . (GHY).
91.44	黃圖	*Huáng tú*	= *Sān fǔ huáng tú* 三輔黃圖, a book about Cháng'ān in the Western Hàn period. The Sān fǔ (B: Three Adjuncts) were the three parts into which the capital region was divided. → line 77.
	禱	*dǎo*	A superstitious action seeking blessings from a god (GHY).
	淫	*yín*	Excessive, immoderate; evil, wicked, vicious; improper relations between the sexes; carnal desires (GHY).
	淫祀	*yínsì*	Non-canonical sacrifices (CY 1831.1).
91.45	徒	*tú*	Anc. *d'uo* (GSR 62e).
	敢	*gǎn*	Anc. *kâm:* (GSR 607a).
	啗	*dàn*	Anc. *d'âm:*, *d'âm-* (GSR 672k).
91.46	未央宮	Wèiyāng Gōng	→ line 57.
91.47	廄	*jiù*	Stable (GHY).
	果下	*guǒxià*	Dwarf (horse or cow) (CY 1544.1, referring to this passage and two others).
92	人臣	*rénchén*	Subject, vassal (CY 158.3).
	臣子	*chénzǐ*	Both a subject and a son; subject (M 9: 387).
	悖	*bèi*	Violate; revolt; false; deceive; confuse (GHY).
	悖亂	*bèiluàn*	To deceive and confuse (CY 1126.1).
	伏	*fú*	→ line 72.

After line 92

92.1	且	*qiě*	. . . ; temporarily (GHY).
	讀奏	*dúzòu*	→ line 72.
92.2	責	*zé, zhài*	→ no. 6 after line 20.

	乖	*guāi*	To violate; inharmonious (GHY).
	布	*bù*	Anc. *puo-* (GSR 102j).
	內	*nèi* *nà*	Anc. *nuậi-* Anc. *nập* (GSR 695e).
	悖	*bó* *bèi*	Anc. *b'uət*, disordered; ample; Anc. *b'uậi-*, disordered (GSR 491d).
93	諸侯	*zhūhóu*	→ line 12.
	侯王	*hóuwáng*	Feudal lords in general (M 1: 766.3).
	列侯	*lièhóu*	→ line 57.
	二千石	*èrqiānshí*	Official Ranking 2000 Shí (B). [cf. line 57].
	綬	*shòu*	Silk ribbon used for carrying seals or jade (GHY).
	墨綬	*mòshòu*	Black silk ribbon tied to the ring of a seal . . . (CY 632.3).
	黃綬	*huángshòu*	Yellow ribbon for a seal . . . (CY 3571.1).

These various ribbons are emblems of specific ranks. See the CY definitions.

	并	*bìng* ...	一起 together; . . . (GHY).
	郎官	*lángguān*	Collective term for *zhōngláng* 中郎, *shìláng* 侍郎, and *lángzhōng* 郎中 (CY 3102.2): Gentleman of the Household, Gentleman in Attendance, Gentleman of the Palace (B).
	免	*miǎn*	→ line 40.
	免奴	*miǎnnú*	\CY \M \HY [Freed slave, see n. 1 after line 101.]
	變易	*biànyì*	To change, replace; . . . (M 10: 615.1).
	旄	*máo*	A banner made of a yak-tail; a large banner; an object made by attaching a yak-tail to a staff, used in giving commands; a yak-tail; a yak (GHY).
94	御府	*yùfǔ*	Imperial Wardrobe (B).

	金錢	*jīnqián*	Metal coinage; (later:) money in general (HY 11: 1185.1).
	采	*cǎi*	. . . ; coloured silk; colour (GHY).
	繒	*zēng*	Silk cloth (in general) (GHY).
	賞賜	*shǎngcì*	To bestow as a reward (M 10: 775.2).
	遊戲	*yóuxì*	→ line 90.
	湛	*zhàn*	Clear, transparent; be full of; heavy; deep; a surname;
		dān	Happy; indulge, wallow (JM).
	湛沔	*dānmiǎn*	To wallow in, indulge in (CY 1841.3).
95	太官	*tàiguān*	→ line 35.
	乘輿	*shèngyú*	Carriage used by Emperor or aristocrats; anything used by the Emperor; any sort of carriage (CY 100.3).
	如故	*rúgù*	As in the past; . . . (M 3: 637.4).
	食監	*shíjiān*	(a) Inspector of Offerings; (b) Inspector of Food (B). (B: *sìjiān*; CY 3421.3: *shíjiān*).
	釋服	*shìfú*	To remove court robes; to remove mourning clothes, i.e. to come out of mourning (CY 3144.2).
	御	*yù*	. . . ; to serve (food etc.) to the ruler (GHY).

It seems clear that *gù* 故 in the two occurrences in this line means "usual" rather than "former", but this meaning is not to be found in the dictionaries.

	趣	*qù, qū*	. . . ;
		cù	To urge, hasten on; quickly (GHY).
	具	*jù*	→ no. 3 after line 38.
	關	*guān*	. . . ; involve, relate to, deal with (GHY). → line 152.
96	豚	*tún*	→ line 84.

	獨夜	*dúyè*	A night spent in solitude; . . . (HY 5: 118.2).
	九賓	*jiŭbīn*	"Commentators are not in agreement on the meaning of *jiŭbīn*" (CY 108.2, which gives three different explanations).
	溫室	*wēnshì*	→ line 65.
97	延見	*yánjiàn*	To receive in audience (M 4: 644).
	姊夫	*zĭfū*	Older sister's husband (CY 747.2, referring to this passage only).
	關內侯	*guānnèi hóu*	Marquis within the Passes (B).
	祖宗	*zŭzōng*	Term of respect for meritorious ancestors (CY 2268.2). . . . ; Founder or restorer of a dynasty (M 8: 434).
	廟祠	*miàocí*	To sacrifice in a temple; a mausoleum (M 4: 614).
	舉	*jŭ*	To lift; to move; to choose, elect; to capture; entirely (GHY).

Wáng Xiānqiān (p. 9a, lines 3–4) indicates that the sacrifice to the dynastic forefathers occurred 36 days after the funeral.

	璽書	*xĭshū*	→ line 18.
	太牢	*tàiláo*	→ line 89.
	祠	*cí*	→ line 89.
	園廟	*yuánmiào*	An ancestor temple in the graveyard of Emperors (CY 578.3).
98	嗣子	*sìzĭ*	Term used by a feudal lord to refer to himself while in mourning; adoptive son (CY 542.1).
	旁午	*pángwŭ*	Crisscrossing; complicated (CY 1388.3).
	旁	*páng*	Broad, outspread; side; perverse, irregular (GHY)
		bàng	. . .
	午	*wŭ*	. . . ; crisscrossing; to resist (GHY).
	官署	*guānshŭ*	Government office (M 3: 967).

	徵發	*zhēngfā*	To draft labour or goods from the people (CY 1091.2).
99	文學	*wénxué*	→ line 78.
	光祿大夫	*guānglù dà-fū*	→ line 8.
	夏侯	Xiàhóu	A surname; . . . (CY 646.3).
	侍中	*shìzhōng*	→ line 7.
	數	*shù, cù, shŭ, shuò*	→ line 30.
	進諫	*jìnjiàn*	To present an admonition (M 11: 91.2).
	過失	*guòshī*	→ line 10.
	簿責	*bùzé*	To send a written official rebuke (CY 2376.2).
	縛	*fù*	To bind (GHY).
	繫獄	*xìyù*	To imprison (CY2470.1).
100	荒淫	*huāngyín*	To neglect one's duty and be lost in comfort and pleasure (CY 2643.2).
	迷惑	*míhuò*	Confused (CY 3052.2).
	帝王	*dìwáng*	Ruler (M 4: 428.4).
	禮誼	*lĭyì*	→ line 80.
	制度	*zhìdù*	General term for statutes and customs (CY 353.3, citing pre-Hàn and Hàn examples); regulations and usage (CY, citing a Yuán example).
	變更	*biàngēng*	To change, reform (M 10: 615.2). *gēng* 更 → line 54.
	以	*yĭ*	. . . ; used like 而 (GHY).
	社稷	*shèjì*	→ line 11.
	雋	*juàn*	. . . ; surname;
		jùn	. . . (CY 3310.1).

After line 101

101.1	免放	*miǎnfàng*	To release, set free; . . . (HY 2: 267.1).
	良人	*liángrén*	A good and honest person; a commoner; 漢女官名; . . . (CY 2607.2).
101.2	劉屈氂	Liú Qūlí	He fought Crown Prince Lì 戾 when he rebelled because of the witchcraft affair, ca. 91 B.C. See Watson, *Courtier and commoner*, p. 49.
	輒	*zhé*	→ line 27.
101.3	沈	*chén*	To sink; to be immersed in; . . . (GHY).
	躭	*dān*	= 耽: large hanging ears; indulge, wallow (in sensual pleasures) (M 10: 973, GHY).
	荒迷	*huāngmí*	To be wild and go astray (M 9: 661.1).
101.4	解脱	*jiětuō*	To excuse, exonerate; . . . (CY 2867.3). To release from shackles; release from prison; . . . (M 10: 367).
101.5	促	*cù*	Urgent; rapid; to urge, press; near; brief (GHY).
101.7	叔孫通傳	*Shūsūn Tōng zhuàn*	The biography of Shūsūn Tōng, *juàn* 43 of the *Hàn shū*. The place referred to here is note 8 on p. 2128.
101.8	喪服	*sāngfú*	→ no. 32 after line 91.
101.9	分布	*fēnbù*	To distribute; to spread out (M 2: 204.1).
	交横	*jiāohéng*	Flowing freely (tears etc.) (M 1: 541.2). Criss-crossing (HY 2: 342.1).
101.10	簿	*bù*	Anc. *b'uo:* (GSR 771o).
	步	*bù*	Anc. *b'uo-* (GSR 73a).
	戶	*hù*	Anc. *γuo:* (GSR 53a).
	文簿	*wénbù*	Official document (CY 1363.1).
	責	*zé, zhài*	→ no. 6 after line 20.
102	雋	*juàn, jùn*	→ line 100.

	高皇帝	Gāo huángdì	Posthumous name of Liú Bāng 劉邦, first Emperor of the Hàn (CY 3479.1, under 高祖).
103	太祖	*tàizǔ*	(Originally:) King Wén of Zhōu 周文王: (later:) an honorific term applied to founders of dynasties (CY 703.3).
	功業	*gōngyè*	Meritorious enterprise (CY 373.2).
	孝文皇帝	Xiào Wén huángdì	Emperor, r. 179–157 B.C.
	慈仁	*círén*	Compassionate, kind-hearted (M 4: 1148).
	節儉	*jiéjiǎn*	Thrifty and economical (CY 2359.2).
	太宗	*tàizōng*	. . . ; honorific title for second Emperor of a dynasty (CY 702.2).
	陛下	*bìxià*	→ line 41.
	孝昭皇帝	Xiào Zhāo huángdì	→ line 16.
	淫辟	*yínpì*	Irregular union between male and female; undisciplined and wicked (CY 1831.2).
	軌	*guǐ*	. . . ; correct (GHY).
	不軌	*bùguǐ*	Immoral, illegal (CY 68.3).

The quotation is from verse 10 of ode no. 256 of the *Shī jīng* 詩經, entitled *Yi* 抑, which has 借 rather than 籍 as the first character. Karlgren translates the line, "You allege that I do not understand, and yet I have carried you in my arms" (*The book of odes*, Göteborg 1950, pp. 218, 219). He argues for this interpretation in "Glosses on the Ta ya and Sung odes" (*Bulletin of the Museum of Far Eastern Antiquities*, 1946, **18**: 106, gloss no. 960). Obviously in the present context Yán Shīgǔ's interpretation (comment no. 3 after line 107) makes more sense, with "you" rather than "I" as the understood subject.

104	籍	*jí*	Archaic *dz'i̯ăk* (GSR 798a′).
	借	*jiè, jié*	Archaic *tsi̯ăg* or *tsi̯ăk* loan, borrow; to allege (GSR 798u).

The Archaic pronunciations are close enough that *jí* 籍 could be used as a phonetic loan for *jiè* 借.

	抱	*bào*	Carry in the arms (GSR 1113j).
	辟	*bì*	Law; lord; to appoint; = 避, to avoid;
		pì	To open up, break ground; to remove; = 僻, remote; wicked; = 譬, for example (GHY).
	五辟	*wǔpì*	= 五刑 (→ no. 4 after line 107); . . . (HY 1: 384).
	周襄王	Zhōu Xiāng wáng	King Xiāng of Zhōu, r. 651–619 B.C.

For the passage from *Chūnqiū* see Couvreur, *Tch'ouen ts'iou*, vol. 1, p. 365; or Legge, *Ch'un ts'ew*, pp. 188, 190, 193.

105	繇	*yáo, yóu*	→ line 32.
	絕	*jué*	To break off, cut off; extremely (GHY).

Wáng Xiānqiān (p. 9b, line 7) comments: "He had not yet been presented [*xiàn* 見] in the temple of Gāozǔ to receive the mandate [*shòu mìng* 受命]".

	可以	*kě yǐ*	→ line 50.
106	天序	*tiānxù*	Genealogy of rulers (CY 685.3).
	祖宗廟	*zǔzōng miào*	→ line 97.
	子	*zǐ*	. . . ; to cherish like one's child (JM).
	萬姓	*wànxìng*	人民 the people (CY 2682.2).
	有司	*yǒusī*	→ no. 6 after line 38.
	御史大夫	*yùshǐdàfū*	→ line 15.
	宗正	*zōngzhèng*	→ line 51.
	太常	*tàicháng*	→ line 75.
	太祝	*tàizhù*	Grand Supplicator (B).
	太牢	*tàiláo*	→ line 89.
	具	*jù*	→ no. 3 after line 38.
107	告祠	*gàocí*	\CY \M \HY

	告祭	*gàojì*	Sacrifice performed extraordinarily at the time of events of great significance to the state (M 2: 909).
	高廟	Gāo Miào	The tomb of Gāozǔ 高祖, founder of the Hàn dynasty (M 12: 616).
	昧死	*mèisǐ*	→ line 79.
	以聞	*yǐwén*	= 上聞, polite formula used in a memorial to the Emperor (M 1: 621.4).

After line 107

107.1	晉灼	Jìn Zhuó	→ no. 1 after line 32.
	辭	*cí*	Anc. *zi* (GSR 968a).
	阮	*ruǎn* *yuán*	Anc. *ngi̯wɒn:* (KXZD 1274, GSR 59h, 256f). Anc. *ngi̯wɒn* (KXZD 1274, GSR 124a, 256a, 257a).
	字	*zì*	Anc. *dz'i-* (GSR 964n).
	雋	*juàn* *jùn*	Anc. *dz'i̯wän:* fat; Anc. *tsi̯uən-* remarkable (GSR 235a).
107.2	僻	*pì*	Remote, far away; wicked, perverse (GHY).
107.3	大雅	*Dà yǎ*	A section of the *Shī jīng* 詩經; . . . (CY 671.2).
	抑	*yì*	To put the hand on, rub; to repress; (self-repressing:) careful, attentive; . . . (GSR 915a).
	衛武公	Wèi Wǔ gōng	Duke Wǔ of Wèi (M 10: 164.4).
	厲王	Lì wáng	King Lì of Zhōu, trad. r. 878–828 B.C.
	假令	*jiǎlìng*	如果 if (CY 241.1).
	幼少	*yòushào*	Young; child (M 4: 530.2).
107.4	五刑	*wǔxíng*	The Five Punishments. In the Qín and Hàn they were: (1) tattooing; (2) cutting off the nose; (3) cutting off the left and right foot; (4) decapitation and display of the head; (5) pickling to make a meat sauce; . . . (HY 1: 350.2).

	頻	*pín*	Anc. *b'i̯ĕn* (GSR 390a).
	亦	*yì*	Anc. *i̯äk* (GSR 800a).
	辟	*bì*	Anc. *pi̯äk* ruler; Anc. *b'i̯äk* law (GSR 853a).
	僻	*pì*	Anc. *p'i̯äk* depraved (GSR 853i).
107.5	惠王	Huì wáng	King Huì of Zhōu, r. 676–652 B.C.
	僖[公]	Xī [gōng]	Duke Xī of Lǔ 魯, r. 658–626 B.C. In the *Chūnqiū* and its commentaries the years are stated as years of the reigns of the Dukes of Lǔ.
	能	*néng*	A kind of bear; able, can; treat well; endure (GSR 885a).
	乎	*hū*	. . . ; in, at, on, at the side of (GSR 55a).
108	起拜	*qǐbài*	To stand and salute (M 10: 838.3).
	受詔	*shòuzhào*	\CY \M \HY
	爭臣	*zhèngchén*	A subject who admonishes his ruler (爭 = 諍 to admonish) (CY 1966.1).
	無道	*wúdào*	Brutal, tyrannical, without benevolence (CY 1931.2).
109	解脱	*jiětuō*	→ no. 4 after line 101.
	璽組	*xǐzǔ*	\CY \M \HY
	組	*zǔ*	. . . ; silk ribbon (GHY).
	扶	*fú*	To support with one's hand; to help; . . . (GHY).
	金馬門	Jīnmǎ Mén	→ line 67.
	奉	*fèng*	→ line 8.
110	隨送	*suísòng*	\ CY \M \HY
	送	*sòng*	. . . ; to see someone off, say farewell to (CY 3051.1).
	愚戇	*yúzhuàng*	Ignorant and without an understanding of reason (CY 1151.2).

	任	*rèn*	. . . ; to be competent, to be able to (GHY).
	就	*jiù*	Near; to reach; even if; to complete (GHY).
	乘輿	*shèngyú*	→ line 95.
	副車	*fùchē*	Carriage of servants of Emperor (CY 362.3).
111	邸	*dǐ*	Hostel in the capital for visiting dignitaries (GHY).

Zì jué yú tiān 自絕於天 is a quotation from *Tàishì* 太誓, one of the forged books of the *Shū jīng* 書經 (CY 2584.3). Legge, *Shoo king*, p. 295: "He has cut himself off from Heaven".

	駑怯	*núqiè*	Stupid and weak (M 12: 509).
	殺身	*shāshēn*	To kill oneself (*Lúnyǔ* 論語: 殺身以成仁) (M 6: 777).
	報德	*bàodé*	To repay another's kindness (CY 617.1).
	寧	*níng*	. . . ;
		nìng	How (rhetorical); would rather (GHY).
	負	*fù*	. . . ; to turn the back on (GHY). → lines 12, 69.
	社稷	*shèjì*	→ line 11.
112	自愛	*zìài*	Self-respect; self-love; selfish (M 9: 403).
	長	*cháng, zhǎng*	→ line 60.
	涕泣	*tìqì*	→ line 12.
	廢放	*fèifàng*	To be removed from office (M 4: 620, citing this passage only).
	屏	*píng, bǐng*	→ no. 43 after line 91.
113	漢中	Hànzhōng	Commandery centred in modern Nánzhèng 南鄭 County, Shǎnxī (CY 1870.1).
	湯沐邑	*tāngmù yì*	Town Which Provides Hot Water for Washing the Hair (B).

	坐	*zuò*	→ line 44.
	亡	*wáng, wàng, wú*	→ line 41.
	輔導	*fŭdăo*	To help and guide (CY 3024.1).
114	陷	*xiàn*	. . . ; to fall into a trap (GHY).
	悉	*xī*	→ line 88.
	誅殺	*zhūshā*	To punish with death (M 10: 464.2).
	號呼	*háohū*	To cry out (M 9: 1080).
	反受	*fănshòu*	\CY \M \HY
	斷	*duàn*	Cut off; bite off; divide; break off, sever; forbid; discontinue; decide, judge; discontinuous; incomplete; absolutely (JM).

After line 114

114.3	侍見	*shìjiàn*	To approach and meet a superior (M 1: 751.3).
114.4	豫	*yù*	. . . ; = *yù* 與, to participate in (GHY).
	政令	*zhènglìng*	Administrative measures and laws (CY 1339.1).
114.5	火	*huŏ*	Anc. *χuâ:* (GSR 353a).
	故	*gù*	Anc. *kuo* (GSR 49g).
	呼	*hū*	Anc. *χuo*, *χuo-* (GSR 55h).
114.6	悔	*huĭ*	To regret (GHY).
115	廣陵王	Guănglíng wáng	→ line 10.
	已前	*yĭqián*	= 以前 (GHY).
	燕刺王	Yān Cì wáng	= Yān wáng Dàn 燕王旦, → line 10.
	誅	*zhū*	→ line 17.
	近親	*jìnqīn*	Close relatives (HY 10: 738.1).

116	衛太子	*Wèi tàizǐ*	→ line 10.
	曾孫	*zēngsūn*	Great-grandson (JM).
	稱述	*chēngshù*	To narrate with praise (M 8: 604, HY 8: 114.1). (Two of M's three examples have 稱述焉)

Line 115ff: There is a somewhat different version of this same passage in the "Annals of Emperor Xuān" 宣帝紀, *Hàn shū, juàn* 8, p. 238; translation Dubs, vol. 2, pp. 204–205.

Dubs is mistaken on where the quotation comes from. See *Lǐ jì* 禮記, *Shísān jīng zhùshū,* p. 1508: 故人道親親也。 親親故尊祖。 尊祖故敬宗。 敬宗故···. This is translated by Legge, *Li ki*, vol. 2, pp. 66–67.

117	祖	*zǔ*	Grandfather; ancestor; . . . (GSR 46b′).
	宗	*zōng*	Ancestor; ancestral temple; . . . (GSR 1003a).

Zǔ and zōng are usually considered to be synonyms, but here the words seem to refer to two distinct kinds of ancestor. The dictionaries don't help. Note 太祖 and 太宗, → line 103.

	大宗	*dàzōng*	In the clan system of the Zhōu, the eldest son of the principal wife and sons succeeding the founder (*shǐzǔ* 始祖) were called *dàzōng* 大宗, and all other sons were called *xiǎozōng* 小宗.
		tàizōng	. . . (CY 665.2).
	支子	*zhīzǐ*	In the feudal clan system, the oldest son of the principal wife, and the sons who succeeded to their ancestors' places, were called *zōngzǐ* 宗子, the others *zhīzǐ* 支子 (CY 1331.1).
118	掖庭	*yètíng*	→ line 90.
	養視	*yǎngshì*	To raise (a child) (M 12: 396).
	至今	*zhìjīn*	Up to now, until now (HY 8: 785.1).
	師受	*shīshòu*	\CY \M \HY
	躬行	*gōngxíng*	Personal behaviour (CY 3012.1).
	節儉	*jiéjiǎn*	→ line 103.

	慈仁	*círén*	→ line 103.
	愛人	*àirén*	Affectionate (M 4: 1127).
	可	*kě*	. . . ; appropriate, suitable (GHY).
119	奉承	*fèngchéng*	To accept; to act in accordance with; to serve; . . . (CY 718.1). Compare lines 105–6: 不可以承天序⋯.
	祖宗廟	*zǔzōngmiào*	→ line 97.
	子	*zǐ*	→ line 106.
	昧死	*mèisǐ*	→ line 79.
	以聞	*yǐwén*	→ line 107.
119	宗正	*zōngzhèng*	→ line 51.
120	里	*lǐ*	Hamlet (division of a prefecture); ward (division of a city) (B). → line 1.
	洗沐	*xǐmù*	To bathe (HY 5: 1153.1).
	御衣	*yùyī*	Clothing of a ruler (HY 3: 1024.2).
	太僕	*tàipú*	→ line 15.
	軨獵車	*línglièchē*	A small hunting carriage (CY 3021.1, referring only to the parallel passage in *juàn* 8).

According to Yán Shīgǔ's comment on the parallel passage in *juàn* 8, a proper Imperial carriage was not ready, and it was necessary to use a smaller carriage. → no. 1 after line 124.

	就	*jiù*	→ line 110.
	齋	*zhāi*	To fast in preparation for a religious ceremony; . . . (GHY).
	就齋	*jiùzhāi*	\CY \HY
121	綬	*shòu*	→ line 93.
	璽綬	*xǐshòu*	Coloured silk ribbon for a seal; a seal (HY 4: 654.2).

	謁	*yè*	To inform, to tell; to request; to pay a formal visit to a superior; . . . (GHY).
	高廟	Gāo Miào	→ line 107.
	孝宣皇帝	Xiào Xuān huángdì	r. 73–49 B.C.
	褒	*bāo*	. . . ; to praise (GHY).
	元功	*yuángōng*	Great achievements (CY 269.3).
	通誼	*tōngyì*	\CY
	通義	*tōngyì*	A generally applicable principle (CY 3063.2).
122	宿衛	*sùwèi*	→ line 37.
	忠正	*zhōngzhèng*	Faithful and honest (M 4: 971).
	宣德	*xuāndé*	To extend virtue (M 3: 998, example 宣德明恩).
	明恩	*míng'ēn*	Excellent grace (M 5: 766).
	守節	*shǒujié*	To abide by one's status and maintain one's moral integrity (CY 802.2).
	秉	*bǐng*	A sheaf of grain; to hold; to control; to administer; power; to inherit; . . . (JM).
	誼	*yì*	→ line 24.
	其	*qí*	. . . ; mood particle indicating a conjecture, rhetorical question, hope, or command (GHY).
	河北	*Héběi*	Hàn prefecture, northeast of modern Ruìchéng County 芮城縣, Shānxī (M 6: 1017).
	東武陽	Dōngwǔyáng	Hàn prefecture, southeast of modern Cháochéng County 朝城縣, Shāndōng (M 6: 194).
123	賞賜	*shǎngcì*	→ line 94.
	斤	*jīn*	→ line 87.
	雜	*zá*	Variegated; . . . (GHY).
	繒	*zēng*	→ line 94.

	雜繒	*zázēng*	\CY \M \HY
	疋	*pǐ*	= 匹. Measure of textiles (in the Hàn, width 二尺二寸, length 四丈); measure for horses (GHY).
124	甲	*jiǎ*	. . . ; to be first or best (GHY).
	第	*dì*	. . . ; large house (JM).
	甲第	*jiǎdì*	Mansion of an aristocrat (CY 2106.2).
	區	*qū*	. . . ; measure for houses (JM).

After line 124

124.1	宣[帝]紀	*Xuān [dì] jì*	"The annals of Emperor Xuān", *juàn* 8 of the *Hàn shū*. The place referred to is on p. 238, with Yán Shīgǔ's comment, no. 3 on p. 239. See also Dubs, vol. 2, p. 205.
125	中郎將	*zhōngláng jiàng*	→ line 52.
	奉車都尉侍中	*fèngchē dūwèi shìzhōng*	[Palace Attendant of the Chief Commandant of Imperial Equipages] (after B). → line 7.
	領	*lǐng*	Collar; measure word, used especially with respect to clothing; to command (GHY).
	壻	*xù*	= 婿 son-in-law (CY 643.1).
	女壻	*nǚxù*	= 女婿 son-in-law; . . . (HY 4: 263.2).
126	衛尉	*wèiwèi*	→ line 19.
	昆	*kūn*	兄 older brother (GHY).
	昆弟	*kūndì*	兄弟 brothers (CY 1407.3).
	外孫	*wàisūn*	Son of a daughter (CY 651.3).
	奉朝請	*fèngcháoqǐng*	Servant at the Spring and Autumn Courts (B).
	諸曹大夫	*zhūcáo dàfū*	[Bureau Grandee] (after B).

	騎都尉	*jìdūwèi*	Chief Commandant of Cavalry (B).
	給事中	*jǐshìzhōng*	→ line 56.
	黨親	*dǎngqīn*	To be intimate with (M 12: 1032, citing this passage only).
	連體	*liántǐ*	To link forms together; blood relations (M 11: 84).
	根據	*gēnjù*	Forcibly occupy, be entrenched (CY 1564.1, citing this passage only).
127	後元	Hòuyuán	→ line 12.
	秉持	*bǐngchí*	Grasp, hold, clasp (M 8: 537).
	萬機	*wànjī*	= 萬幾, a ruler's numerous and complex daily government affairs (CY 2683.2, 2682.3).
	歸政	*guīzhèng*	To return political power (HY 5: 372.1).
	謙讓	*qiānràng*	To yield modestly (M 10: 554).
	關白	*guānbái*	To report (to a superior); . . . (CY 3253.3).
	奏御	*zòuyù*	To inform the Emperor (M 3: 587).
128	朝見	*cháojiàn*	To appear in audience with the Emperor (M 5: 1059).
	虛己	*xūjǐ*	Modest, not complacent (CY 2751.1).
	斂容	*liǎnróng*	To make one's appearance solemn (CY 1356.1).
	禮下	*lǐxià*	\CY \M \HY
	已甚	*yǐshèn*	Exaggerated (HY 4: 72.1).

After line 128

128.1	下、胡、稼	*xià, hú, jià*	→ no. 6 after line 38.
129	秉政	*bǐngzhèng*	To hold political power (M 8: 537).
	地節	Dìjié	Reign period, 69–66 B.C.
	篤	*dǔ*	Serious (of an illness) (GHY).

	病篤	*bìngdǔ*	→ line 12.
	車駕	*chējià*	→ line 64.
	臨問	*línwèn*	To investigate personally and extend sympathy (CY 2581.2).
	涕泣	*tìqì*	→ line 12.
	謝恩	*xièēn*	To express gratitude for someone's kindness (CY 2914.1).
130	國邑	*guóyì*	In the Hàn period, a fief; . . . (M 3: 73).
	票騎將軍	*piāojì jiāngjūn*	→ line 1.
	丞相	*chéngxiàng*	→ line 51.
	御史	*yùshǐ*	→ line 57.
	奉	*fèng*	→ line 8.
	祀	*sì*	To offer sacrifices (JM).
	奉祀	*fèngsì*	To offer sacrifices (HY 2: 1508.2).
132	薨	*hōng*	To die (of a nobleman) (GHY).
	喪	*sāng, sàng*	→ line 82.
	太中大夫	*tàizhōng dà-fū*	→ line 79.
	侍御史	*shìyùshǐ*	Attending Secretary (B).
	持節	*chíjié*	To hold the tallies, i.e. to be responsible (CY 1250.2).
	護	*hù*	To control, to govern (GHY).
	喪事	*sāngshì*	Funeral; coffin (HY (3: 408.2).
	中二千石	*zhòng èr-qiānshí*	→ line 57.
133	莫府	*mùfǔ*	→ line 36.
	冢	*zhǒng*	→ no. 42 after line 91.

	金錢	*jīnqián*	→ line 94.
	繒絮	*zēngxù*	Silk clothing (CY 2468.2). 繒 → line 94.
	繡	*xiù*	Embroidery (GHY).
	被	*bèi, pī*	→ line 70.
	領	*lǐng*	→ line 125.
	篋	*qiè*	A small box (GHY).
	璧	*bì*	A jade disk with a hole in the middle (GHY).
	珠	*zhū*	A pearl; a bead (JM).
	璣	*jī*	不圓的珠子 a non-round bead (GHY).
	玉衣	*yùyī*	Clothing embellished with jade; beautiful clothes in general; shroud for ruler; . . . (HY 4: 478.1).
	梓宮	*zǐgōng*	"Catalpa palace", coffin of an Emperor (GHY).
	便房	*biànfáng*	In the mausoleum of an Emperor or King, a small room used by the officiants at the funeral (CY 213.2, referring to this passage).
	黃腸	*huángcháng*	"Yellow intestines", an outer coffin made of yellow heartwood of cypress (CY 3570.2, referring to this passage).
	題湊	*tícòu*	Outer coffin for nobleman, made by piling up large logs (CY 3397.3).

Archaeological investigations in the last few years have clarified the construction of imperial and princely tombs, making passages like this easier to understand. See e.g. Wáng Zhòngshū, *Han civilization*, pp. 175–179.

134	樅木	*cōngmù*	Type of tree, probably cryptomeria (CH 2920).
	臧	*zāng*	. . . ;
		zàng	= 藏 (JM). → no. 4 after line 136.
	椁	*guǒ*	= 槨, outer coffin (JM).

	東園	*dōngyuán*	A Hàn office in charge of supplying objects for Imperial tombs (CY 1528.3). Eastern Garden (B).
	東園溫明	*dōngyuán wēnmíng*	Ancient type of coffin (CY 1532.3, referring to this passage).
	乘輿	*shèngyú*	→ line 95.
	制度	*zhìdù*	→ line 100.
	柩	*jiù*	→ no. 34 after line 91.
	尸柩	*shījiù*	Coffin (HY 4: 2.2).
	載	*zài, zǎi*	→ line 83.
	轀輬車	*wēnliángchē*	Sleeping carriage (CY 3030.1).
135	黃屋	*huángwū*	Canopy of Imperial or royal carriage (CY 3568.2).
	纛	*dào*	Banner on Imperial carriage; . . . (CY 2478.2).
	左纛	*zuǒdào*	= *dào* 纛, term is used because the banner was flown on the left side of the carriage (CY 959.3, citing this passage only).
	材官	*cáiguān*	Skilled Soldier (B).
	北軍	*běijūn*	Northern Army (B).
	五校士	*wǔxiàoshì*	Troops of the Five Colonels (B).
	軍陳	*jūnzhèn*	Military formation (HY 9: 1209.2).
	茂陵	Màolíng	A Hàn prefecture, near modern Xīngpíng County 興平縣, Shǎnxī; name of the mausoleum of Wǔ-dì 武帝, also in Xīngpíng County; . . . (HY 9: 333.2). See *Wénwù* 文物, 1976.7: 87–89; Wáng Zhòngshū, *Han civilization*, pp. 211–212.
	送葬	*sòngzàng*	To accompany a coffin to the place of burial (HY 10: 811.1).
	諡	*shì*	→ line 60.

	三河	Sān Hé	The three commanderies Hénèi 河內, Hénán 河南, and Hédōng 河東, i.e. the region north and south of the Yellow River in the vicinity of Luòyáng; . . . (CY 29.3).
	穿	*chuān*	. . . ; to dig (JM).
136	復土	*fùtǔ*	Grave fill (CY 1085.3).
	冢	*zhǒng*	→ no. 42 after line 91.
	祠堂	*cítáng*	Temple for offerings to ancestors or to the wise and meritorious (CY 2267.3).
	園邑	*yuányì*	Dwelling area for those who maintain a mausoleum (CY 578.2).
	長	*zhǎng*	Chief (B).
	丞	*chéng*	Assistant (B).
	奉守	*fèngshǒu*	To serve and protect (M 3: 582).

After line 136

136.1	典	*diǎn*	→ line 82.
136.2	漢儀	*Hàn yí*	A book on the ritual usages of the Hàn, written by Shūsūn Tōng 叔孫通 in the Western Hàn and revised by Cáo Bāo 曹褒 in the Eastern Hàn; . . . (M 7: 225.3).
	襦	*rú*	→ line 71.
	鎧	*kǎi*	Armour (GHY).
	連綴	*liánzhuì*	To string together; to narrate (HY 10: 869.2).
	縷	*lǚ*	Thread (GHY).
	要	*yào*	. . . ;
		yāo	= 腰, waist (JM).
	已下	*yǐxià*	= 以下 GHY).
	札	*zhá*	. . . ; leaves of armour (GHY).

	尺、寸	*chǐ, cùn*	→ line 21.
136.4	服虔	Fú Qián	According to Yán Shīgǔ's preface (p. 4), he lived in the Later Hàn period.
	藏	*zàng*	. . . ; to bury; funeral mound (HY 9: 591.1).
	便坐	*biànzuò*	To sit in a separate room: a separate rom, a wing of a house (HY 1: 1362.2).
	柏木	*bǎimù*	Cupressus funebris (CY 1552.1, CH 2946).
	累	*lěi*	Multiple, in layers; . . . (GHY).
	題	*tí*	. . . ; 端 end (JM).
	湊	*còu*	To collect, gather; to flee to (GHY).
	中明	*zhōngmíng*	\CY \HY
	丈	*zhàng*	10 *chǐ* 尺; . . . (JM). → line 21.
	曲室	*qūshì*	Deeply secret room (CY 1456.1).
	楩	*pián*	Large tree of south China (CY 1609.3, CH 3016).
136.5	婢妾	*bìqiè*	Concubine; maidservant (CY 760.3).
	廚廄	*chújiù*	An office, first established in the Hàn period, which administered the kitchen and stables of the establishment of the Empress and the Crown Prince; . . . (M 4: 609.4). Kitchen, Stables (two separate offices) (B). [It appears that Morohashi and Bielenstein interpret a sentence in *Hàn shū* differently, *juàn* 19a, p. 734.]
	樅木	*cōngmù*	→ line 134.
	柏	*bǎi*	→ no. 4 after line 136.
	松	*sōng*	General term for Pinaceae (CH 2920).
	檜	*guì*	A kind of evergreen tree (GHY). Sabina chinensis (CH 2968).
	七	*qī*	Anc. *ts'i̯ĕt* (GSR 400a).
	庸	*yōng*	Anc. *i̯wong* (GSR 1185x).

	樅	*zōng*	Anc. *tsi̯wong*
		cōng	Anc. *ts'i̯wong* (GSR 1191i).
	檜	*guì*	Anc. *kwâi-*
		guo	Anc. *kuât* (GSR 321i).
	工	*gōng*	Anc. *kung* (GSR 1172a).
	闊	*kuò*	Anc. *k'uât* (GSR 302q).
	栝	*guo*	Anc. *kuât* (GSR 302i). [More common modern pronunciations are *guā* and *kuò*, CY 1566.1, CH 2967].
136.6	處	*chù*	. . . ;
		chǔ	. . . ; to keep; 處理 to deal with, to process (JM).
	漆	*qī*	Lacquer; . . . (CY 1873.3).
	桶	*tǒng*	A square measuring vessel; a cylindrical vessel (CY 1580.2).
	懸	*xuán*	To suspend; . . . (CY 1177.2).
	屍	*shī*	Corpse (CY 910.2).
	斂	*liǎn*	To receive, collect; to collect (taxes); . . . ;
		liàn	To dress and lay a corpse in a coffin (GHY).
	大斂	*dàliàn*	To clothe a corpse is called 小斂; to lay a corpse in the coffin is called 大斂 (CY 676.1).
	并蓋	*bìnggài*	\CY
	少府	*shàofǔ*	→ line 51.
136.7	文穎	Wén Yǐng	→ no. 2 after line 20.
	輀	*ér*	= 輀 a funeral carriage (M 10: 1068).
	喪輀車	*sāngérchē*	\CY \HY
	衣車	*yīchē*	→ line 83.
	窗牖	*chuāngyǒu*	Window (HY 8: 446.2).
	涼	*liáng*	= 凉 cool; . . . (JM).

	臣瓚	Chénzàn	Yán Shīgǔ in his preface (p. 5) says that he knows neither this man's surname nor anything else about him.
	駕	*jià*	→ line 64.
	大廄	*dàjiù*	Great Stables (B).
	駟	*sì*	A team of four horses (JM).
	倅	*cuì*	Auxiliary; deputy (GHY).
	安車	*ānchē*	A type of carriage in which one can ride sitting down (HY 3: 1317.1, including an illustration from a Hàn tomb relief). See also Hayashi, p. 331.
	柳	*liǔ*	Willow; canopy on a funeral carriage ; . . . (JM).
	翣	*shà*	A kind of coffin decoration; . . . (CY 2507.2).
	柳翣	*liǔshà*	A kind of coffin decoration (HY 4:930.1).
	密閉	*mìbì*	Tightly sealed (HY 3: 1537.2).
	各別	*gèbié*	Each separately; . . . (HY 2: 180.1).
	載	*zài, zǎi*	→ line 83.
	喪	*sāng, sàng*	→ line 82.
	載喪	*zàisāng*	\HY
	藩飾	*fānshì*	Decoration, pattern (HY 9: 608.1).
	千	*qiān*	Anc. *ts'ien* (GSR 365a).
	內	*nèi* *nà*	Anc. *nuậi* Anc. *nập* (GSR 695e).
	倅	*cuì*	Anc. *ts'uậi* (GSR 490d).
136.8	高[帝]紀	*Gāo[dì] jì*	"The annals of Emperor Gāo", *juàn* 1 of the *Hàn shū*. The reference here is to *juàn* 1a, pp. 40–41, note 2. See also Dubs, vol. 1, pp. 40–41 and fn. 1 on p. 41.
137	樂平	Lèpíng	Hàn prefecture and marquisate, modern Tángyì 堂邑 County, Shāndōng (DM 1167.1).

	以	*yǐ*	→ line 1.
	奉車都尉	*fèngchē dūwèi*	→ line 7.
	領尚書事	*lǐng shàng-shū shì*	Intendant of the Masters of Writing (B). [Here presumably: To act as Intendant of the Masters of Writing.]
	功德	*gōngdé*	Achievements and virtues; . . . (HY 2: 770.2).
	故	*gù*	→ line 68.
138	宿衛	*sùwèi*	→ line 37.
	遭	*zāo*	To encounter; . . . (GHY).
	大難	*dà'nàn*	. . . ; difficulties (CY 676.2).
	秉、誼	*bǐng, yì*	→ line 122.
	三公	*sāngōng*	Three Excellencies . They were the Chancellor (*chéngxiàng* 丞相), the Grandee Secretary (*yùshǐ dàfū* 御史大夫), and the Grand Commandant (*tàiwèi* 太尉) (B, pp. 7–10).
	九卿	*jiǔqīng*	→ line 30.
	大夫	*dàfū*	→ line 57.
139	冊	*cè*	. . . ; = 策 plan, strategem (GHY).
	萬世冊	*wànshìcè*	\CY \M \HY
	蒸庶	*zhēngshù*	The common people (CY 2699.1).
	以	*yǐ*	. . . ; used like 已 (JM).
	康寧	*kāngníng*	Peaceful and untroubled (CY 1012.1).
	茂盛	*màoshèng*	Flourishing (M 9: 598).
	復	*fù*	. . . ; to release from taxes and corvée labour (GHY).
	疇	*chóu*	Ploughed field; good field; category; to equalise; . . . (JM).
	爵邑	*juéyì*	Rank and fiefs (HY 6: 1114.2).

140	與	*yŭ, yù, yú*	→ line 85.
	相國	*xiàngguó*	Chancellor of State (B).

The reference is to Xiāo Hé 蕭何, d. 193 B.C., earliest chancellor of the Hàn, who is usually credited with much of the work of its foundation (*Cambridge history*, p. 108).

	外祖父	*wài zŭfù*	Maternal grandfather (M 3: 332).

Xŭ Guănghàn 許廣漢 "had served as a courtier to the king of [Chāngyì 昌邑], and owing to a mistake or accident he had the misfortune to suffer the punishment of castration." Loewe, *Crisis and conflict*, p. 124.

	平恩	Píng'ēn	Hàn marquisate, modern Qiūxiàn 丘縣 County, Hébĕi (DM 212.3).
141	忠正	*zhōngzhèng*	→ line 122.
	勤勞	*qínláo*	Anxious, worried; fatigued, weary; meritorious service (HY 2: 819.2).
	其	*qí*	→ line 122.
	中郎將	*zhōngláng jiàng*	→ line 52.
	冠陽	*guānyáng*	\CY \DM \HY \M

After line 141

141.1	應劭	Yīng Shào	According to Yán Shīgŭ's preface (p. 4) he was a man of the Later Hàn period.
	等	*dĕng*	Equal; rank, grade; step, layer; category; compare; . . . (JM).
	方	*fāng*	Anc. *pi̯wang* (or *b'wâng*) (GSR 740a).
	目	*mù*	Anc. *mi̯uk* (GSR 1036a).
	復	*fù*	Anc. *b'i̯uk*, return; Anc. *b'i̯ə̯u-*, repeat (GSR 1034d).

The Ancient reading *b'wâng* for 方 is for an unusual meaning, and it would have been odd to use it in a sound gloss. The reading for 復 intended by the commentator is probably *pi̯uk*, which, like the two readings listed above, becomes *fù* in modern Běijīng pronunciation.

141.2	豫	*yù*	→ no. 4 after line 114.
141.3	褒寵	*bāochǒng*	To praise and love (M 10: 260). 褒 = 褎.
142	太夫人	*tàifūrén*	Mother of a nobleman (CY 706.1).
	時	*shí*	. . . ; 那時，當時 at that time (GHY).
	塋	*yíng*	Land for a tomb (GHY).
	制	*zhì*	To cut (wood); sanction, punish; forbid; control, manage; to lead; correct, put right; stipulate; 制度 system; method; command of a ruler; scale, dimensions; funeral of father or mother; . . . (JM).
	塋制	*yíngzhì*	\HY
	侈大	*chǐdà*	. . . ; to expand (HY 1: 1344.1, citing only this passage).
	闕	*què*	. . . ; stelae on both sides in front of a tomb (GHY).
	出闕	*chūquè*	\CY \M \HY
	神道	*shéndào*	. . . ; entranceway to a tomb (CY 2273.2).
143	昭靈	*Zhāolíng*	Name of a palace in the Hàn period (M 5: 842, citing this passage and its commentary only).
	承恩	*Chéng'ēn*	. . . ; name of a palace in the Hàn period (M 5: 119.2, citing this passage and its commentary only).
	祠室	*císhì*	= 祠堂, mausoleum; shrine (M 8: 464). → line 136.
	輦	*niǎn*	→ line 65.
	輦閣	*niǎngé*	A covered walkway (HY 9: 1283.2).
	通屬	*tōngzhǔ*	To be joined, to communicate (M 11: 64).

	永巷	*yǒngxiàng*	A long lane in the Hàn palace, restricted to women; the harem; . . . (CY 1715.2). Long Lanes (B).
	幽	*yōu*	. . . ; to imprison (GHY).
	良人	*liángrén*	→ no. 1 after line 101.
	婢妾	*bìqiè*	→ no. 5 after line 136.
	治	*zhì*	. . . ; to build (JM).
	第室	*dìshì*	Residence, mansion (M 8: 762).
	乘輿	*shèngyú*	→ line 95.
144	繡	*xiù*	→ line 133.
	絪馮	*yīnpíng*	Cushion in a carriage (HY 9: 823.1, citing this passage only).
	塗	*tú*	→ no. 43 after line 91.
	韋絮	*wéixù*	Leather and silk wadding, used on axle as shock absorber (M 12: 186, citing this passage only).
	絮	*xù*	Coarse silk floss; to pad clothing with silk floss (GHY).
	薦	*jiàn*	. . . ; straw mat; to pad, to cushion (GHY).
	侍婢	*shìbì*	Maidservant; female slave (HY 1: 1316.2).
	輓	*wǎn*	To pull, lift; . . . (JMG).
	游戲	*yóuxì*	To romp and play; . . . (HY 5: 1510.2). Note 遊戲, → line 90.
	第	*dì*	→ line 124.
	愛幸	*àixìng*	To love and trust unduly (a subordinate) (CY 1152.1).
	監奴	*jiānnú*	Slave responsible for domestic affairs (CY 2190.2).
145	馮	*féng*	A surname;
		píng	. . . (JM).

計事	*jìshì*	To record a superior's actions; . . . (HY 11: 60.2).
寡居	*guǎjū*	To be a widow (CY 857.2).
繕治	*shànzhì*	Put in order, repair (HY 9: 1021.2).
第宅	*dìzhái*	Upper-class residence (CY 2350.1).
馳逐	*chízhú*	To chase at a gallop; to pursue; to race horses (M 12: 501).
平樂館	Pínglè Guǎn	Name of a Hàn palace (HY 2: 943.1).
146 朝請	*cháoqǐng*	In the Hàn law codes, the noblemen's spring audience with the Emperor was called *cháo* 朝, while the autumn audience was called *qǐng* 請; . . . (CY 1490.3).
稱病	*chēngbìng*	To feign illness (HY 8: 115.1).
圍	*wéi*	To encircle; to surround; defensive wall; circumference; measure word (GHY). . . . ; hunting grounds; animal pen (CY 577.3, citing late examples).
張圍	*zhāngwéi*	\CY \M \HY
圍獵	*wéiliè*	To surround and hunt (CY 577.3, citing only a very late example, from *Jīn shǐ* 金史).
黃山	Huángshān	A Hàn palace, in modern Xīngpíng 興平 County, Shǎnxī; . . . (HY 12: 969.1).
蒼頭	*cāngtóu*	. . . ; "blue-head", i.e. a slave (slaves wore blue turbans) (CY 2701.2).
朝謁	*cháoyè*	To present oneself in audience at the domicile of the ruler (M 5: 1056).
莫	*mò*	. . . ; 沒有甚麼，沒有誰 (GHY).
譴	*qiǎn*	To reproach, reprove, blame (GHY).
長信宮	Chángxìn Gōng	→ line 77.
期度	*qīdù*	Limit (CY 1487.3, citing this passage and one other).

After line 147

147.2	服虔	Fú Qián	→ no. 4 after line 136.
	李奇	Lǐ Qí	Yán Shīgǔ's preface (p. 4) has no more information about him than that he came from Nányáng 南陽.
	冢	*zhǒng*	→ no. 42 after line 91.
	冢園	*zhǒngyuán*	\CY \M \HY
	墓園	*mùyuán*	A park with a tomb (HY 2: 1167.1).
	文穎	Wén Yǐng	→ no. 2 after line 20.
147.3	掖庭	*yètíng*	→ line 90.
147.4	茵	*yīn*	Mat (GHY).
	蓐	*rù*	Mat (GHY).
	茵馮	*yīnpíng*	Cushions and rests in a carriage; carriage seats (M 9: 626).
	輿輦	*yúniǎn*	Carriage of the Emperor (M 10: 1051).
147.5	緣	*yuán*	Fringe on clothing; along; to follow; to borrow (GHY).
	著	*zhù, zhuó*	→ no. 2 after line 43.
	取	*qǔ*	→ line 87.
	搖動	*yáodòng*	To rock, sway, shake (CY 1300.2).
	張	*zhāng*	Anc. *t̂i̯ang* (GSR 721h).
	呂	*lǚ*	Anc. *li̯wo:* (GSR 76a).
	著	*zhù* *zhuó*	Anc. *t̂i̯wo-*; Anc. *t̂i̯ak*, place, put, apply; Anc. *d̂'i̯ak*, attach (K45n′).

Ancient *t̂i̯wo:* gives modern Běijīng *zhǔ* (e.g. GSR 45g).

147.7	漢語	*Hàn yǔ*	→ no. 1 after line 32.

	東閭	Dōnglǘ	→ no. 1 after line 32.
	代立	*dàilì*	To succeed to the throne (CY 170.3).
	素	*sù*	. . . ; always, constantly (GHY).
	監知	*jiānzhī*	Supervise, manage (HY 7: 1447.1).
147.8	才	*cái*	Anc. *dz'ậi* (GSR 943a).
	姓	*xìng*	Anc. *si̯äng-* (GSR 812q).
	請	*qǐng* *qíng*	Anc. *ts'i̯äng:*; Anc. *dz'i̯äng* (GSR 812k′).

Ancient *dz'i̯äng-* gives modern Běijīng *jìng* (e.g. GSR 811d).

147.9	謁	*yè*	. . . ; visiting card (GHY). → line 121.
	上謁	*shàngyè*	To request an audience (CY 63.2).
	通名	*tōngmíng*	To send one's visiting card, asking for a meeting; . . . (M 11: 66).
148	聞知	*wénzhī*	To hear about, be aware of; . . . (HY 12: 105.1).
	尊盛	*zūnshèng*	→ line 28.
	日久	*rìjiǔ*	For a long time (HY 5: 537.2).
	薨	*hōng*	→ line 132.
	躬親	*gōngqīn*	To do by oneself; by oneself (M 10: 972).
	朝政	*cháozhèng*	To administer court affairs; . . . (HY 6: 1318.2).
	給侍中	*jǐshìzhōng*	→ line 56.
149	女	*nǚ*	. . . ;
		rǔ	= 汝 you (JM).
	曹	*cáo*	. . . ; plural suffix translateable with 們 (GHY).
	女曹	*rǔcáo*	\CY \HY
	汝曹	*rǔcáo*	你們 you (plural) (HY 5: 940.1).

	務	*wù*	To devote oneself to; matter, affair; must (GHY).
	奉	*fèng*	→ line 8.
	餘業	*yúyè*	Family estate/merit/etc. passed down through generations.
	大夫	*dàfū*	→ line 57.
	給事中	*jǐshìzhōng*	→ line 56.
	他人	*tārén*	Others (HY 1: 1155.1).
	壹	*yī*	→ line 16.
	間	*jiān*	. . .
		jiàn	. . . ; to separate, disconnect (GHY).
	壹間	*yījiàn*	\CY \HY
150	爭道	*zhēngdào*	. . . ; to fight over the right of way (HY 2: 600.1).
	欲	*yù*	. . . ; 將要 be about to (JM).
	蹹	*tà*	To trample; . . . (GHY). = 蹋.
	叩頭	*kòutóu*	→ line 6.
151	知	*zhī*	. . . ; to perceive, be conscious of; to feel (GHY).
	知憂	*zhīyōu*	\CY \M \HY
	燕見	*yànjiàn*	To have audience in private (M 7: 531).
	言事	*yánshì*	To discuss matters of state with the ruler; . . . (HY 11: 5.2).
	侍中	*shìzhōng*	→ line 7.
	徑出	*jìngchū*	To appear in person (M 4: 868).
	省	*shěng*	. . . ; office
		xǐng	. . . (GHY).
152	自若	*zìruò*	Self-possessed, calm; 依然如故 as originally (HY 8: 1316.1, M 9: 409).

	領尚書 [事]	*lǐng shàng-shū [shì]*	Intendant of the Masters of Writing (B).
	吏民	*lìmín*	Local officials and common people (M 2: 839).
	封事	*fēngshì*	A sealed memorial (CY 869.19.

The matter of the two sealed envelopes for memorials to the Emperor is described in the Annals of Emperor Xuān, *Hàn shū*, *juàn* 8, translation Dubs, vol. 2, p. 218.

	關	*guān*	→ line 95.

After line 153

153.1	輩	*bèi*	. . . ; 等 and others (JM).
	汝輩	*rǔbèi*	你們 you (plural) (HY 5: 940.1).
153.2	居	*jū*	Anc. *ki̯wo* (GSR 49c′).
	莧	*xiàn*	Anc. *γăn-* or *γwan:* (GSR 241h).
	間	*jiān* *jiàn* *xián*	Anc. *kăn*, crevice, space; Anc. *kăn-*, to separate; Anc. *γăn*, leisure (GSR 191b).
153.4	告語	*gàoyǔ*	To inform: . . . (M 2: 909).
153.5	如故	*rúgù*	→ line 95.
154	微	*wēi*	. . . ; of humble position (GHY).
	妃	*fēi*	Spouse; wife of emperor, second in rank to empress; principal wife of a crown prince or feudal lord; . . . ;
		pèi	婚配 to marry (JM).
	乳醫	*rǔyī*	Corresponds roughly to a gynaecologist and obstetrician (CY 116.3, citing this passage only).
	淳于	Chúnyú	A surname (HY 5: 1408.1).
	行	*xíng*	. . . ; to give (CY 2799.1, with an example from *Lǐ jì* 禮記).

	毒藥	*dúyào*	A type of medicine; a type of poison (CY 1694.2, citing early examples for both meanings).
155	勸	*quàn*	To encourage, urge; . . . (GHY).
	內	*nèi, nà*	→ line 27.
	外戚傳	*Wàiqī zhuàn*	"Accounts of families related to the Emperors by marriage", *juàn* 97 of the *Hàn shū*. Excerpts are translated in Watson, *Courtier and commoner*, pp. 247–278.
	暴崩	*bàobēng*	Sudden death of Emperor or Empress (HY 5: 827.1).
	捕	*bǔ*	→ line 19.
	劾	*hé*	To expose guilt (GHY).
	侍疾	*shìjí*	To attend the sick (HY 1: 1315.2).
	亡狀	*wúzhuàng*	Improper (CY 149.1).
	不道	*bùdào*	Improper; . . . (CY 71.1).
	下獄	*xiàyù*	Send to prison (HY 1: 329.1).
156	簿	*bù*	Records, archives (GHY).
	簿問	*bùwèn*	\M HY (8: 1268.1) quotes this passage and one from a Qīng text, but does not take a position on what it means. Presumably something like: to interrogate for the record.
	急	*jí*	Impatient; urgent; urgent need; quick; to reduce, tighten (GHY).
	敗	*bài*	. . . ; fail (JM).
	語	*yǔ*	To discuss; to converse; to narrate; speech; . . . ;
		yù	To tell, inform (JM).
	發舉	*fājǔ*	To rise, stage an uprising; to expose, inform against (HY 8: 574.1).
	猶與	*yóuyù*	To hesitate (CY 2006.2).

	署	*shǔ*	→ no. 37 after line 91.
157	論	*lùn*	. . . ; to convict (of a crime) (GHY).
	稍	*shāo*	→ line 7.
	泄	*xiè*	→ line 91.
	察	*chá*	To investigate; to see clearly; . . . (GHY).
	女壻	*nǚxù*	→ line 125.
	度遼將軍	*dù Liáo jiāngjūn*	→ line 73.
158	衛尉	*wèiwèi*	→ line 19.
	光祿勳	*guānglùxūn*	Superintendant of the Imperial Household (B).
	諸吏	*zhūlì*	→ line 78.
	中郎將	*zhōngláng jiàng*	→ line 52.
	羽林[左右]監	*yǔlín [zuǒ, yòu] jiān*	Inspector of the [Left, Right] of the Feathered Forest (B). 羽林 → line 35.
	安定	Āndìng	A Hàn commandery, in modern Gānsù (CY 804.3).
	姊婿	*zǐxù*	Elder sister's husband (CY 747.2). 婿 → line 126.
159	給事中	*jǐshìzhōng*	→ line 56.
	光祿大夫	*guānglù dàfū*	→ line 8.
	蜀郡	Shǔ jùn	A Hàn commandery, in modern Sìchuān (CY 2769.1).
	太守	*tàishǒu*	→ line 4.
	孫婿	*sūnxù*	Husband of granddaughter (CY 793.1).
	武威	Wǔwēi	A Hàn commandery, in modern Gānsù (CY1671.1).
	頃之	*qǐngzhī*	→ line 70.

160	少府	*shàofǔ*	→ line 51.
	冠	*guān, guàn*	→ line 40.
	小冠	*xiǎoguān*	In ancient times, a hat which was smaller than usual in height and breadth (HY 2: 1613.2, giving several text examples which unfortunately do not seem to help in determining what its significance was).
	綬	*shòu*	→ line 93.
	屯兵	*túnbīng*	Guard troops; . . . (HY 1: 485.2).
	官屬	*guānshǔ*	Subordinate official (CY 824.1).
	特	*tè*	Alone; only; . . . (JM).
161	俱	*jù*	→ line 64.
	散騎	*sànjì*	Cavalier Attendant (B).
	騎都尉	*jìdūwèi*	Chief Commandant of Cavalry (B).
	領胡越騎	*lǐng Hú Yuè jì*	\B \HY [Intendant of Hú and Yuè Cavalry].
	胡騎	*Hú jì*	Hu Cavalry (B).
	越騎	*Yuè jì*	Picked Cavalry (B) [??] A cavalry composed of assimilated Yuè tribesmen (HY 9: 1116.2).

After line 163

163.1	產乳	*chǎnrǔ*	Childbirth (HY 7: 1519.2).
	而	*ér*	Anc. *ńźi* (GSR 982a).
	樹	*shù*	Anc. *źi̯u-*, tree Anc. *źi̯u:*, to plant (GSR 127j).
	乳	*rǔ*	Anc. *ńźi̯u:* (GSR 135a).
163.2	步	*bù*	Anc. *b'uo-* (GSR 73u).
	戶	*hù*	Anc. *γuo:* (GSR 53a).

	簿	*bù*	Anc. *b'uo:* (GSR 771o).
163.6	但	*dàn*	Only, exclusively; . . . (GHY).
164	大司馬	*dàsīmǎ*	→ line 14.
	稱病	*chēngbìng*	→ line 146.
	故	*gù*	→ line 68.
	長史	*zhǎngshǐ*	→ line 36.
	候問	*hòuwèn*	To call upon someone; to inquire about someone's health (M 1: 833).
	縣官	*xiànguān*	Prefectural officials; the court of the Emperor (CY 2457.2).
165	墳墓	*fénmù*	Place of interment. In ancient times a grave with a mound was called a *fén* 墳, while a grave without a mound was called a *mù* 墓 (CY 629.1).
	乾	*qián*	. . . ;
		gān	Dry (GHY).
	印綬	*yìnshòu*	A seal and its ribbon; official rank (HY 2: 518.1).
	不省	*bùxǐng*	Without investigating;
		bùshěng	Without economizing (CY 69.1).
	恨望	*hènwàng*	Resentment, hate (CY 1118.2).
166	權柄	*quánbǐng*	Power, authority (CY 1649.2).
	廷尉	*tíngwèi*	→ line 68.
	种	*chóng*	(CY 2300.3). [*Not* the modern simplified character for *zhǒng* 種!]
	左馮翊	*Zuǒpíngyì*	→ line 77.
167	車丞相	Chē chéng-xiàng	Cancellor Chē, i.e. Chē Qiānqiū 車千秋, also known as Tián Qiānqiū 田千秋. See Loewe, *Crisis and conflict*, esp. p. 68.
	少府	*shàofǔ*	→ line 51.

	坐	*zuò*	. . . ; to be convicted of; because (GHY).
	逆	*nì*	→ line 17.
	逆意	*nìyì*	To go against the wishes of a superior; a rebellious will; to anticipate (HY 10: 832.1).
	小家子	*xiǎojiā zǐ*	A person of humble origin (HY 2: 1617.2, citing only this passage).
	得幸	*déxìng*	→ line 3.
168	九卿	*jiǔqīng*	→ line 30.
	百官	*bǎiguān*	Officialdom, the bureaucracy (HY 8: 231.2).
	但	*dàn*	→ no. 6 after line 163.
169	怨恨	*yuànhèn*	→ line 34.
	愚	*yú*	Stupid; polite first person pronoun (GHY).
	默	*mò*	Calm; silent; dark; corrupt (CY 3580.2).
	默然	*mòrán*	Silent (HY 12: 1344.1).
	視事	*shìshì*	To attend to one's official duties (CY 2854.2).

After line 169

169.2	疏斥	*shūchì*	To shun and spurn (M 7: 1148.2).
169.3	自省	*zìxǐng*	To examine oneself (CY 2584.1).
169.6	沖	*chōng*	(CY 1738.3).

169.7 The reference is to line 76.

169.9	象似	*xiàngsì*	Appearance (HY 10: 17.1).
170	侵削	*qīnxuē*	To bully and humiliate (CY 215.1).
	啼泣	*tíqì*	To weep (HY 3: 436.1).
	自怨	*zìyuàn*	Remorseful (HY 8: 1322.1).
	用事	*yòngshì*	. . . ; to be in office, to hold power; in season (CY 2100.2).

	縣官	*xiànguān*	→ line 164.
	變易	*biànyì*	→ line 93.
171	法令	*fǎlìng*	General term for laws, regulations, etc.; . . . (HY 5: 1036.1).
	公田	*gōngtián*	. . . ; fields owned by the State (CY 311.3).
	賦與	*fùyǔ*	To give, allot (M 10: 770).
	發揚	*fāyáng*	. . . ; to proclaim, spread (CY 2153.2).
	過失	*guòshī*	→ line 10.
	儒生	*rúshēng*	A Confucian scholar (HY 1: 1712.1).
	窶	*jù*	Poor, impoverished (GHY).
	遠客	*yuǎnkè*	A guest from afar; a traveller from a far-off country; . . . (M 11: 153).
	飢寒	*jīhán*	Hungry and cold (M 12: 377, citing numerous examples).
172	妄說	*wàngshuō*	Absurd opinions (M 3: 642).
	狂言	*kuángyán*	Wildly arrogant talk; ravings of a sick person; boasting (CY 1995.1).
	忌諱	*jìhuì*	Taboo words or actions (CY 1100.3).
	常	*cháng*	→ line 83.
	讎	*chóu*	To reply; to correspond to; to sell; enemy; to hate (GHY).
	使	*shǐ*	. . . ; 使用 to use (GHY).
	對事	*duìshì*	對質 to confront (in court); appropriate, matching (HY 2: 1298.1).
173	專制	*zhuānzhì*	→ line 31.
	擅權	*shànquán*	Dictatorship, monopoly (CY 1316.2).
	用事	*yòngshì*	→ line 170.
	昆弟	*kūndì*	→ line 126.

	驕恣	*jiāozì*	Arrogant and self-indulgent (CY 3467.2).
	宗廟	*zōngmiào*	→ line 54.
174	災異	*zāiyì*	Natural disaster (CY 1915.1).
	絕	*jué*	→ line 105.
	痛	*tòng*	Painful; thorough (GHY).
	屏	*píng, bǐng*	→ no. 43 after line 91.
	黠	*xiá*	Sly, tricky; intelligent (GHY). = 黠.
	封事	*fēngshì*	→ line 152.
	輒	*zhé*	→ line 27.
	中書令	*zhōngshū lìng*	Prefect of the Palace Writers (after B).
175	廉正	*liánzhèng*	Honest and upright (CY 1016.1).
176	謹	*jǐn*	→ line 68.
	讙	*huān*	Confused noise; . . . (GHY).
	讙言	*huānyán*	Noisy rumours (HY 11: 465.1).
	昆弟	*kūndì*	→ line 126.
	壻	*xù*	→ line 125.
	恐急	*kǒngjí*	Alarmed (HY 7: 491.2, citing this passage only).
177	離散	*lísàn*	To separate, disperse; to loosen (HY 11: 892.1).
	斥逐	*chìzhú*	To drive out, banish (CY 1371.2).
178	誅罰	*zhūfá*	To punish for a crime (M 10: 465).
	邪謀	*xiémóu*	Conspiracy, intrigue (M 11: 225).

After line 178

178.1	無禮	*wúlǐ*	Not following correct etiquette; impolite (HY 7: 158.1).

	其	*jí* *jì* *qí*	Anc. *kji*; Anc. *kji-*; Anc. *g'ji* (GSR 952a).
	羽	*yǔ*	Anc. *ji̯u:* (GSR 98a).
	窶	*jù*	Anc. *g'i̯u:* (GSR 123o).
178.2	許	*xǔ*	Anc. *χi̯wo:* or *χuo:* (GSR 60i).
	吏	*lì*	Anc. *lji-* (GSR 975g).
	喜	*xǐ*	Anc. *χji:* (GSR 955a).
178.3	嫉	*jí*	To envy, be jealous of; to hate (GHY).
	仇讎	*qiúchóu*	Personal enemy (CY 166.1).
	爰	*yuán*	Anc. *ji̯wɒn* (GSR 255a).
	讙	*huān* *xuān*	Anc. *χuân*; Anc. *χi̯wɒn* (GSR 158n).
179	天官	*tiānguān*	An official post (pre-Hàn); officials in general; astronomy; sense organs; . . . (CY 686.2).
	語	*yǔ, yù*	→ line 156.
	熒惑	*yínghuò*	To dazzle; the planet Mars (CY 1946.2).
	守	*shǒu*	. . . ; (of a planet:) to enter the domain of (a star) (HY 3: 1296.1).
	御星	*yùxīng*	\CY \M \HY
	太僕	*tàipú*	→ line 15.
	奉車都尉	*fèngchē dūwèi*	→ line 7.
	黜	*chù*	To banish; to remove; to reduce (GHY).
180	舅	*jiù*	Mother's brother; husband's father; = 外舅 wife's father; wife's brother; . . . (CY 2592.3).
	善	*shàn*	. . . ; be on friendly terms with (JM).
	卒卒	*cùcù*	→ line 68.

	用事	*yòngshì*	→ line 170.
181	太夫人	*tàifūrén*	→ line 142.
	[皇]太后	*[Huáng] Tàihòu*	→ line 51.
	移徙	*yíxǐ*	To move; to transplant, respectful term for moving domicile (M 8: 575).
	男子	*nánzǐ*	Boy; man; male (M 7: 1079).
	廷尉	*tíngwèi*	→ line 68.
	執金吾	*zhíjīnwú*	→ line 76.
182	捕	*bǔ*	→ line 19.
	縣官	*xiànguān*	→ line 164.
	竟	*jìng*	→ no. 5 after line 43.
183	端	*duān*	An end or a side of a thing; a beginning; aspect; proper, correct; . . . (GHY).
	惡端	*èduān*	\CY \M \HY
	弑	*shì*	To kill a superior (GHY).
	寬仁	*kuānrén*	Broad of mind and deep of compassion (M 3: 1107).
	猶	*yóu*	Monkey; resemble; still, yet; 尚且 even (GHY).
	族	*zú*	. . . ; an ancient punishment, execution of the three or nine sets of relatives (GHY).
	不如	*bùrú*	Not as good as (GHY).
184	安所	*ānsuǒ*	To live peacefully; where? (HY 3: 1319.2).
	避	*bì*	To hide; to avoid (GHY).

After line 184

184.1	曉	*xiǎo*	Daybreak; to know, understand; to notify (GHY).
	星文	*xīngwén*	Astrological phenomena; . . . (HY 5: 671.1).

184.2	猝	*cù*	→ no. 1 after line 72.
	忽遽	*cōngjù*	Hastily, suddenly (CY 1129.3). 忽 = 匆.
184.3	難	*nán*	. . . ; = 戁, to fear, dread (GHY).
	窮	*qióng*	Blocked; unsuccessful; impoverished; limit, end; to investigate thoroughly (GHY).
	窮竟	*qióngjìng*	→ no. 5 after line 43.
184.5	受禍	*shòuhuò*	To suffer calamity (HY 2: 886.1).
185	無禮	*wúlǐ*	→ no. 1 after line 178.
	坐	*zuò*	→ line 167.
	交通	*jiāotōng*	To be in contact; to associate; to collaborate, conspire (CY 151.2).
	辭	*cí*	. . . ; statement made by the accused under interrogation (GHY).
	宿衛	*sùwèi*	→ line 37.
	免	*miǎn*	→ line 40.
	就第	*jiùdì*	To leave office and return to one's home (M 4: 119).
	遇	*yù*	. . . ; to meet; to treat (GHY).
186	犯法	*fànfǎ*	To violate regulations, laws, or commands (HY 5:6.2).
	讓	*ràng*	→ line 20.
	第	*dì*	→ line 124.
	溢	*yì*	Overflow; full; excessive; . . . (GHY).
	溢流	*yìliú*	To overflow (HY 6: 38.1).
	庭	*tíng*	Hall; courtyard; . . . (JM).
	竈	*zào*	Stove; god of the stove; name of a ceremony (GHY). = 灶.

	居	*jū, jī*	→ line 83.
187	捕	*bǔ*	→ line 19.
	不	*bù*	. . . ;
		fǒu	= 否 (GHY).
	亟	*jí*	Quickly;
		qì	Repeatedly (GHY).
	鼠	*shǔ*	Mouse, rat; . . . (CY 3593.1).
	暴	*pù*	Dry; exposed;
		bào	Fierce and sudden; vicious; damage; . . . (GHY).
	觸	*chù*	To butt with horns; to collide; to touch, move; to offend (GHY).
	鴞	*xiāo*	A violent ferocious bird (GHY).
188	尚冠	Shàngguān	A ward (*lǐ* 里) in Cháng'ān in the Hàn (HY 2: 1661.2).
	里	*lǐ*	→ line 120.
	宅	*zhái*	Residence; to reside; . . . (JM).
	巷	*xiàng*	Alley, lane; a residence (CY 965.3).
	端	*duān*	→ line 183.
	屋	*wū*	House, dwelling; anything covered; ancient measure of length (CY 910.3).
	徹	*chè*	To penetrate; thorough; to remove; to withdraw; to demolish (GHY).
189	亡有	*wúyǒu*	沒有 not have, not exist (HY 2: 294.2). 亡 → line 41.
	車騎	*chējì*	Carriage and horses; you (polite form of address); chariots and warhorses (corresponding to modern cavalry); abbr. of *chējì jiāngjūn* 車騎將軍 (→ line 14); ancient name of a star (HY 9: 1197.1).
	讙	*huān*	→ line 176.

正	*zhèng*	. . . ; expresses continuity of movement (GHY, giving example from Hàn shū: 正讙不可止).
舉	*jǔ*	→ line 97.
憂愁	*yōuchóu*	Distressed and grieved (M 4: 1176).
擅	*shàn*	→ line 36.
減	*jiǎn*	To reduce; less than; to damage; to punish, kill (JM).
羔	*gāo*	Small sheep; . . . (CY 2494.1).
菟	*tú*	. . . ;
	tù	= 兔, hare, rabbit (CY 2673.3).
190 鼃	*wā*	Kind of frog (CY 3587.3).
可以	*kě yǐ*	→ line 50
191 承	*chéng*	→ line 50.
制	*zhì*	→ line 142.
承制	*chéngzhì*	To act on Imperial orders (CY 1228.2).
引	*yǐn*	. . . ; 取過來 to seize (GHY).
斬	*zhǎn*	→ line 61.
約定	*yuēdìng*	Agreement, covenant (M 8: 941).
拜	*bài*	→ line 15.
玄菟[郡]	Xuántù [jùn]	Commandery, on the border between modern Jílín and Korea (DM 232.2).
太守	*tàishǒu*	→ line 4.
太中大夫	*tàizhōng dàfū*	→ line 79.
代郡	Dài jùn	Commandery, modern Yùxiàn 蔚縣 County, Hébĕi (DM 179.2, CY 170.3).

192	寫	*xiě*	. . . ; to copy; to overflow; [the meaning "to write" is found only in the Táng period and after];
		xiè	= 瀉, to pour out; diarrhoea (GHY).
	祕書	*mìshū*	Important secret documents; official title (HY 7: 902.1).
	獻	*xiàn*	To offer in sacrifice; to offer as tribute to a superior; . . . (GHY).
	贖	*shú*	. . . ; to redeem a punishment by payment or service (GHY).
	報聞	*bàowén*	To reply that what was reported is already known; = 報罷, to anounce that a memorial has not been accepted; . . . (CY 616.3).
	發覺	*fājué*	→ line 46.
193	要斬	*yāozhǎn*	→ line 91.
	昆弟	*kūndì*	→ line 126.
	棄市	*qìshì*	To execute in the marketplace and display the corpse in the street (CY 1585.2).
	唯獨	*wéidú*	Only, alone (HY 3: 388.1).
	處	*chǔ*	To reside at, to be at (a certain place); to hold, keep; to stay; . . .
		chù	A place (JM). → no. 6 after line 136.
	昭臺宮	Zhāotái gōng	A hall in the Park of the Supreme Forest (Shànglín yuàn 上林苑, → 91.43) (HY 5: 689.2).
194	連坐	*liánzuò*	Persons punished along with the actual perpetrator of a crime (CY 3057.2).
	誅滅	*zhūmiè*	To annihilate as punishment for a crime (M 10: 465).

After line 194

194.1	自以	*zìyǐ*	\CY \HY

	姨母	*yímŭ*	Mother's sisters: 姨 can mean either mother's sisters or wife's sisters, and 母 is added to specify the meaning (CY 751.1, citing this comment only).
194.2	總	*zŏng*	. . . ; entirely (GHY).
	責	*zé, zhài*	→ no. 6 after line 20.
194.4	且	*qiĕ*	. . . ; 將要，快要 be about to (GHY).
	亟	*jí* *qì*	Anc. *ki̯ək*, urgently; Anc. *k'ji-*, often (GSR 910a).
	居	*jū*	Anc. *ki̯wo* (GSR 49c′).
	力	*lì*	Anc. *li̯ək* (GSR 928a).
194.5	室	*shì*	→ line 39.
	屋	*wū*	→ line 188.
	室屋	*shìwū*	\HY
	通	*tōng*	. . . ; entirely, generally (JM).
	黃霸傳	*Huáng Bà zhuàn*	The biography of Huáng Bà, *juàn* 89 of *Hàn shū.* The place cited here is on page 3632, with Yán Shīgŭ's comment no. 2 on p. 3633.
	羽	*yŭ*	Anc. *ji̯u:* (GSR 98a).
	驕	*jiāo* *qiāo* *xiāo*	Anc. *ki̯äu*; Anc. *k'i̯äu*; Anc. *χi̯äu* (GSR 1138o).
	鴞	*xiāo*	Anc. *ji̯äu* (GSR 1041t).
194.6	擅議	*shànyì*	To plan and decide arbitrarily (M 5: 405, citing two examples from Hàn shū, both concerned with Imperial sacrifices).
	供祭	*gòngjì*	To allot for use in sacrifices (M 1: 756).
194.7	外祖母	*wàizŭmŭ*	Maternal grandmother (M 3: 332.1).
195	乃者	*năizhĕ*	In the past (CY 97.2).
	東織室令史	*dōng zhīshì lìngshĭ*	[Foreman Clerk of the Eastern Weaving House] (B).

	魏郡	Wèi jùn	A Hàn commandery, near modern Línzhāng County 臨漳縣, Héběi (DM 1339.1).
	豪	*háo*	Outstanding person; powerful person; . . . (GHY).
	冠陽	Guānyáng	→ line 141.
	大逆	*dànì*	Great evil deeds such as killing a ruler or father or ruining ancestor temples or Imperial tombs (M 3: 386).
196	抑	*yì*	To press down, opposite of yáng 揚; to inhibit, hold back; . . . (GHY).
	冀	*jì*	To hope (GHY).
	自新	*zìxīn*	To correct one's own faults and renew oneself (CY 2584.3).
	從昆	*cóngkūn*	\CY \M \HY
	昆弟	*kūndì*	→ line 126.
	從弟	*cóngdì*	堂弟 younger male cousin with same surname (HY 3: 1006.1).
	從子	*cóngzǐ*	Brother's son (HY 3: 1003.2).
	弟子	*dìzǐ*	Younger brothers and sons; young men in general; . . . (HY 2: 100.1).
197	姊妹	*zǐmèi*	Older and younger sisters; . . . (HY 4: 310.2).
	壻	*xù*	→ line 125.
	姊壻	*zǐxù*	→ line 158.
	妹壻	*mèixù*	Younger sister's husband (HY 4: 314.2).
	詿誤	*guàwù*	To mislead (CY 2890.1).
	賴	*lài*	To rely on (GHY).
	宗廟	*zōngmiào*	→ line 54.
	神靈	*shénlíng*	General term for gods; soul; . . . (HY 7: 891.2).
	先發	*xiānfā*	The first to start (HY 2: 244.1).

	伏	*fú*	. . . ; to receive (punishment) (GHY). → line 72.
	辜	*gū*	Punishment; to break the limbs in punishment (GHY).
198	悼	*dào*	Sorrowful; to mourn (GHY).
	丙申	*bǐngshēn*	Day no. 33 in the 60-day cycle.
	發覺	*fājué*	→ line 46.
	赦除	*shèchú*	To grant pardon to (M 10: 824).
	語	*yǔ, yù*	→ line 156.
	期門	*qīmén*	→ line 71.
199	左曹	*zuǒcáo*	Bureau Head of the Left (B).
	侍中	*shìzhōng*	→ line 7.
	召見	*zhàojiàn*	→ line 29.
	對狀	*duìzhuàng*	To testify (CY 880.2).
	以聞	*yǐwén*	→ line 107.
	建	*jiàn*	. . . ; 建議 to propose, recommend (GHY).
	禁闥	*jìntà*	→ line 8.
	卒	*zú*	→ line 68.
	讎	*chóu*	To respond; to sell; enemy; to hate; . . . (GHY).
	博成	Bóchéng	\DM
	高昌	Gāochāng	A Hàn marquisate, modern Bóxīng County 博興縣, Shāndōng (DM 773.4).
	平通	Píngtōng	\DM
	都成	Dūchéng	(Not a place name in the Hàn period) (DM 948.3, 949.1).
	樂陵	Lèlíng	Hàn marquisate, modern Lèlíng County, Shāndōng (DM 1169.2).

After line 201

201.1	宣[帝]紀	*Xuān [dì] jì*	→ no. 1 after line 124.
201.3	立意	*lìyì*	Intention, purpose; to propose; . . . (HY 8: 377.2).
201.5	等類	*děnglèi*	. . . ; equal (HY 8: 1142.2).
202	奢侈	*shēchǐ*	Extravagance, waste (CY 725.2).
	茂陵	Màolíng	→ line 135.
	奢	*shē*	Extravagance, excess (GHY).
	遜	*xùn*	To escape; to yield; modest; slightly inferior (GHY).
	侮	*wǔ*	To slight, treat without proper respect (GHY).
	逆道	*nìdào*	A way which is contrary to correct principles (M 11: 44).
203	害	*hài*	To injure; to kill; disaster; to hate (GHY).
	秉權	*bǐngquán*	To be in control of political power (HY 8: 32.1).
	日久	*rìjiǔ*	→ line 148.
204	待	*dài*	To wait, wait for; to treat; to guard against (GHY).
	何待	*hédài*	How could it happen that . . . (rhetorical negative) (HY 1: 1230.1, giving only a modern example).
	疏	*shū, shù*	→ line 21.
	泰	*tài*	Excessively; 最 most; . . . (GHY).
	愛厚	*àihòu*	To favour, to be intimate with (M 4: 1126).
	以時	*yǐshí*	Within a specified time; promptly, immediately (HY 1: 1091.1).
	抑制	*yìzhì*	To restrain, repress, stop (M 5: 132). 抑 → line 196.
	輒	*zhé*	→ line 27.
	報聞	*bàowén*	→ line 192.

205	主人	*zhŭrén*	Master, proprietor; many people; one who works for himself; you (M 1: 333).
	誅滅	*zhūmiè*	→ line 194.
	過	*guò*	. . . ; to visit (JM).
	竈	*zào*	→ line 186.
	突	*tū*	. . . ; chimney (JM).
	直突	*zhítū*	Straight chimney (M 8: 166, citing this passage only).
206	不	*bù, fŏu*	→ line 187.
	火患	*huŏhuàn*	Calamity caused by fire (CY 1911.1).
	嘿	*mò*	= 默, to close the mouth and not speak (CY 549.3).
	俄	*é*	Slanted; an instant (GHY).
	俄而	*éér*	不久 not long afterward (GHY).
	失火	*shīhuŏ*	To catch fire and burn; . . . (HY 2: 1478.2).
	鄰	*lín*	. . . ; nearby (GHY).
	里	*lǐ*	→ line 120.
	救	*jiù*	To stop; help; rescue; . . . (JM).
	幸而	*xìng'ér*	Luckily (HY 2: 1089.1).
	息	*xī*	. . . ; to stop (GHY).
	灼爛	*zhuólàn*	To be burned (M 7: 377).
208	錄	*lù*	→ line 18.
	鄉使	*xiàngshǐ*	假如 if, supposing that (HY 10: 663.2). 鄉 = 向 or 嚮.
209	恩澤	*ēnzé*	→ no. 3 after line 32.
	燋	*jiāo*	Torch; to be injured by fire;
		qiáo	. . . (GHY).

	爛	*làn*	. . . ; to be injured by fire (JM).
	額	*é*	Forehead; . . . (GHY).
	寤	*wù*	To wake up; to realize one's error, wake up to reality (GHY).
	且	*qiě*	→ no. 4 after line 194.
	變	*biàn*	→ no. 6 after line 25.
210	防絕	*fángjué*	To guard against and break off contact with (M 11: 794).
	裂土	*liètǔ*	To divide up land by enfeoffment; . . . (HY 9: 69.1).
	逆亂	*nìluàn*	To revolt and be disorderly (M 11: 44).
	誅滅	*zhūmiè*	→ line 194.
	敗	*bài*	. . . ; damage, destruction (GHY).
	往事	*wǎngshì*	Affairs of the past (CY 1068.2).
211	蒙	*méng*	. . . ; to receive; to suffer (GHY).
	唯	*wéi*	. . . ; sentence adjunct indicating wish, desire (GHY).
	焦	*jiāo*	Damage by fire (CY 1936.2).
	灼爛	*zhuólàn*	→ line 206.

After line 212

212.2	被	*bèi, pī*	→ line 70.
	燒炙	*shāozhì*	To bake, roast, grill, etc. (M 7: 525).
	胡	*hú*	Anc. *γuo* (GSR 49a′).
	浪	*láng* *làng*	Anc. *lâng*; Anc. *lâng-* (GSR 735k).
	郎	*láng*	Anc. *lâng* (GSR 735r).

	行	*xíng*	Anc. *γɒng*, road; walk;
		háng	Anc. *γâng*, rank, row;
		hàng	Anc. *γâng* or *γâng-*, strong, vigorous (GSR 748a).
212.3	嚮	*xiàng*	To face; to hasten toward; to approach; in the past; if, supposing that; window;
		xiǎng	享受 to enjoy (GHY).
213	謁見	*yèjiàn*	To be presented to a superior (M 10: 546).
	高廟	Gāo miào	→ line 107
	驂乘	*cānchéng*	To ride on the right in a carriage; = *péichéng* 陪乘, to act as a bodyguard on a carriage (CY 3465.3, 3273.2).
	嚴憚	*yándàn*	To fear and be awed by (M 2: 1179).
	芒	*máng*	Thorn; point of a knife; rays of light; . . . (GHY).
	刺	*cì*	To stab, prick; a sharp, needle-like object; . . . (GHY).
	芒刺	*mángcì*	Awn (of grain); thorn (M 9: 523).
	芒刺在背	*mángcì zài bèi*	Foreboding, dread (CY 2615.1, citing this passage as the source of the expression).
214	從容	*cōngróng*	Free and easy; activity; . . . (CY 1082.2).
	肆體	*sìtǐ*	To relax and be at ease (M 9: 244).
	安近	*ānjìn*	Comfortable and intimate (HY 3: 1318.1).
	竟	*jìng*	→ no. 5 after line 43.
	威震	*wēizhèn*	To cause to tremble with fear (M 3: 703).
215	畜	*chù*	Domestic animals;
		xù	To raise (domestic animals); to accumulate (GHY).

After line 215

215.1	鉅	*jù*	Anc. *g'i̯wo:* (GSR 95r).
	靳	*jìn*	Anc. *ki̯ən-* (GSR 443e).

	近	*jìn*	Anc. *g'i̯ən:*, near; Anc. *g'i̯ən-*, to be near to (GSR 443g).
216	成帝	Chéng-dì	Emperor, r. 32–8 B.C.
	守冢	*shǒuzhǒng*	Tomb caretaker (HY 3: 1304.1).
	吏卒	*lìzú*	Official troops; petty officials and official employees (HY 1: 521.2).
	奉祠	*fèngcí*	Offer sacrifices; . . . (HY 2: 1511.1).
	元始	Yuánshǐ	Reign period, A.D. 1–5.
	從父	*cóngfù*	Older or younger brother of father (HY 3: 1003.2).
	昆弟	*kūndì*	→ line 126.
216	曾孫	*zēngsūn*	→ line 116.

218–285 No glosses are provided here for lines 218–285, the biography of Jīn Mìdī 金日磾.

286	贊	*zàn*	To lead; to assist; an acolyte; to narrate; to praise; a literary genre, often rhymed, used in praise; to eulogise (JM).
	結髮	*jiéfà*	"Binding the hair", ancient ritual for a boy's coming of age (JM).
	內侍	*nèishì*	To serve within the Imperial palace; . . . (HY 1: 1004.1).
	階闥	*jiētà*	"Palace stairways and doors". i.e. palace chambers (HY 11: 1061.2).
	確然	*quèrán*	Staunch, unyielding; faithful (HY 7: 1095.1).
	秉志	*bǐngzhì*	Firm of purpose (HY 8: 30.1).
	誼	*yì*	→ line 24.
	形	*xíng*	. . . ; to show, manifest (JM).
	襁褓	*qiǎngbǎo*	A broad belt for carrying an infant and a quilt for swaddling it; a swaddled infant; general term for infants and children (HY 9: 139.2).

	託	*tuō*	To entrust to the care of (JM).
287	寄	*jì*	→ line 59.
	當	*dāng*	. . . ; take responsibility for (JM).
	廟堂	*miàotáng*	A hall in the Imperial Ancestral Temple; the Imperial court; . . . (HY 3: 1275.2).
	擁	*yōng*	To carry in the arms; to hold; to surround; crowded; to obstruct; to protect; to possess; to conceal; to support, endorse (JM).
	幼君	*yòujūn*	A young ruler (HY 4: 430.2).
	摧	*cuī*	To snap, break; to destroy; to foil, defeat; to ridicule; sorrowful (JM).
	燕王	Yān wáng	→ line 10.
	仆	*pū*	To fall forward; to fall (JM). To fall forward; push over, overturn; fall dead; cause to be defeated; declining, decadent; . . . (HY 1: 1103.1).
	制	*zhì*	→ line 142.
	處	*chǔ, chù*	→ line 193.
	廢置	*fèizhì*	Appointment and removal of officials; enthronement and dethronement of rulers; . . . (HY 1282.2).
	際	*jì*	Margin, borderline; between; . . . (JM).
	臨	*lín*	→ line 86.
	大節	*dàjié*	Law and order; matter of life and death; . . . (HY 2: 1383.2).
288	可奪	*kěduó*	\HY
	奪	*duó*	Take by force; eliminate; lose; drop; to choose to accept or reject; to dazzle; a narrow road (JM).
	匡	*kuāng*	. . . ; 正 to correct, rectify (examples: *Shījīng*: 以匡王國; *Lúnyǔ*: 一匡天下) (JM).
	社稷	*shèjì*	→ line 11.

	昭	Zhāo	→ line 16.
	宣	Xuān	→ line 121.
	師保	*shībǎo*	An ancient [pre-Hàn] office in charge of advising the ruler and educating the children of the royal family; teachers in general; education (HY 3: 720.1).
	周公	Zhōu gōng	→ line 12.
	阿衡	*ēhéng*	A Shàng officer with advisory and educational duties; term used to refer to Yī Yǐn 伊尹 (→ 54), who held this post; in general, one who assists a ruler, the Chancellor (HY 11: 938.1).
288	術	*shù*	. . . ; 學術 learning (JM).
	闇	*àn*	Dark; ignorant; . . . (HY 12: 133.1).
	大理	*dàlǐ*	. . . (HY 2: 1367.2).
	陰	*yīn*	. . . ; to hide (HY 11: 1017.2).
	邪謀	*xiémóu*	→ line 178.
	湛	*zhàn, dān*	→ line 94.
	湛溺	*zhànnì*	To flood, inundate; to indulge; to sink into, fall into (HY 5: 1443.1).
	盈溢	*yíngyì*	To overflow; abundant; indulgent (example is this passage); to suffuse, cover everywhere (HY 7: 1419.1).
	顛覆	*diānfù*	Disordered; to fall, drop; to be defeated; to overturn, topple; tired out, exhausted (HY 12: 350.2).
	財	*cái*	→ line 21.
	宗族	*zōngzú*	→ line 46.
290	誅夷	*zhūyí*	Massacre, slaughter (HY 11: 171.2).
	霍叔	Huò Shū	A younger brother of King Wû of Zhōu 周武王, also known as Huò Shūchù 霍叔處 (M 12: 57.2).

	河東	Hédōng	The region of modern Shānxī province (HY 5: 1057.1). → line 1.
	豈	*qǐ*	難道 do you really mean that . . . ; how (rhetorical); it may be that . . . ; should, used like 其;
		kǎi	. . . (JM).
	苗裔	*miáoyì*	Descendant (HY 9: 338.2).
	金日磾	Jīn Mìdī, Jīn Mītī	→ before line 1.
	夷狄	*yídí*	Ancient collective term for non-Chinese ethnic groups; peripheral regions occupied by non-Chinese ethnic groups (HY 2: 1496.2).
	亡國	*wángguó*	(Of a ruler:) to lose one's state; a defeated state; a state destined to be defeated (HY 2: 297.1).
	羈虜	*jīlǔ*	To take prisoner and detain (HY 8: 1057.2).
	漢庭	*Hàn tíng*	The Hàn court (HY 6: 50.2).
291	篤敬	*dǔjìng*	Loyal and respectful (HY 8: 1224.1).
	寤	*wù*	→ line 209.
	忠信	*zhōngxìn*	Faithful and trustworthy (HY 7: 416.2).
	自著	*zìzhù*	\HY
	著	*zhù, zhuó*	→ no. 2 after line 43.
	勒功	*lègōng*	To inscribe a person's achievememts on stone; to establish meritorious service (HY 2: 797.2).
	上將	*shàngjiàng*	Principal general, commander; name of a star (HY 1: 287.2).
	後嗣	*hòusì*	Later generations; descendants (HY 3: 967.2).
	內侍	*nèishì*	→ line 286.
292	休屠	Xiūtú	The Buddha (example from the *Hàn shū* biography of Huò Qùbìng 霍去病: 收休屠祭天金人. Yán Shīgǔ's comment: 今之佛像是也); . . . (M 1: 666.2).

	祭天	*jìtiān*	To sacrifice to heavenly gods, or to Heaven (HY 7: 910.2).
	故因	*gùyīn*	\HY
	賜姓	*cìxìng*	Bestowal by the ruler of a surname based on a person's ancestors' place of origin or special accomplishments (HY 10: 261.1).
	云	*yún*	. . . ; it is said that (sentence suffix) (JM).

After line 292

292.2	頓	*dùn*	→ line 13.
	仆	*fù* *pòu* *fòu* *bo*	Anc. *p'i̯u-* Anc. *p'ə̯u-* Anc. *p'i̯ə̯u-* Anc. *b'ək* Fall prostrate (GSR 1210g).
	赴	*fù*	Anc. *p'i̯u* (GSR 1210i).
292.3	伊尹	Yī Yǐn	→ line 55.
	官號	*guānhào*	Official title (HY 3: 1393.2).
	倚	*yǐ*	Depend on; rely on; according to; to lean to one side; . . .
		jī	Monstrous, strange (JM).
	群下	*qúnxià*	→ line 59.
	取	*qǔ*	. . . ; to choose; to seek out (HY 2: 871.1). → line 87.
	沈	*chén*	→ no. 3 after line 101.
	沈溺	*chénnì*	To sink in water; to fall into (a predicament); a difficult situation; to sink into; to indulge, wallow in; rheumatism (HY 5: 1009).
292.6	纔	*cái*	→ no. 1 after line 25.
	文王	Wén Wáng	King Wén of Zhōu, father of King Wǔ 武王 (CY 507.2).
	武王	Wǔ Wáng	King Wǔ of Zhōu, conqueror of Shāng and founder of the Zhōu empire (CY 507.3).

Index

chén 沈 101.3
chén 陳 64
chéng 丞 136
chéng 承 50
chēngbì 稱蹕 35
chēngbìng 稱病 146
Chéng-dì 成帝 216
Chéng'ēn 承恩 143
Chéngmíng 承明 64
chēngshù 稱述 116
chéngxiàng 丞相 51
chéngzhì 承制 191
chénjìng 沈靜 21
chénliè 陳列 71
chénnì 沈溺 292.3
Chénzàn 臣瓚
136.7
chénzhuàng 陳狀 64
chénzǐ 臣子 92
chí 持 48
chǐ 尺 21
chì 敕 68
chíbīng 持兵 71
chǐdà 侈大 142
chíjié 持節 132
chízhú 馳逐 145
chìzhú 斥逐 177
chūquè 出闕 142
chōng 沖 169.6
chóng 种 166
Chónghé 重合 17
chǒngjī 寵姬 10
chōngshí 充實 47
chóu 疇 139
chóu 讎 172, 199
chǔ 處 136.6, 193
chǔ 礎 63.2
chù 畜 215
chù 處 136.6, 193
chù 黜 179
chù 觸 187
chuān 穿 135
chuáng 牀 15
chuāngyǒu 窗牖
136.7
chújiù 廚廏 136.5
Chúnyú 淳于 154
cí 祠 89
cí 慈 80
cí 辭 185
cì 次 84, 91.36
cì 刺 213
cì 賜 12
círén 慈仁 103
cítáng 祠堂 136
cíxiào 慈孝 80
cìxìng 賜姓 292
cóngdì 從弟 196
cóngfù 從父 216
cōngjù 怱遽 184.2
cóngkūn 從昆 196
cōngmù 樅木 134
cōngróng 從容 214
cóngshì 從事 18
cóngzhōng 從中 37
cóngzǐ 從子 196
còu 湊 136.4
cù 卒 68
cù 促 101.5
cù 數 30
cù 趣 95
cù 猝 72.1
cuī 縗 91.32
cuī 衰 91.43
cuī 摧 287
cuì 倅 136.7
cuīcháng 縗裳
91.32
cuīdié 衰絰 91.43
cùn 寸 21

dà hónglú 大鴻臚
51
dà sīnóng 大司農
53
Dà yǎ 大雅 107.3
dàfū 大夫 57
dài 待 204
Dài jùn 代郡 191
dàilì 代立 147.7
dàjiāngjūn 大將軍
14
dàjié 大節 287
dàjiù 大廏 136.7
dàlǐ 大理 288
dàliàn 大斂 136.6
dān 躭 101.3
dān 湛 94
dān 酖 20
dàn 但 163.6
dàn 啗 89
dà'nàn 大難 138
dāng 當 13, 37, 287
dǎngqīn 黨親 126
Dāngtú 當塗 74
dāngyǔ 當與 38
dǎngyǔ 黨與 44
dànì 大逆 195
dānmiǎn 湛沔 94
dǎo 禱 91.44
dào 悼 198
dào 纛 135
dàsīmǎ 大司馬 14
dàxíng 大行 84
dàzōng 大宗 117
dé 得 61
dé 德 28
děng 等 141.1
děnglèi 等類 201.5
déxìng 得幸 3
dézuì 得罪 69
dí 嫡 32.1
dǐ 邸 111
dì 第 124
diǎn 典 82
diǎn sāngfú 典喪服
82
diǎn shǔguó 典屬國
36
diānfù 顛覆 288
diào 調 36
diāohuà 彫畫 43.1

jūnzhèn 軍陳 135
jūsāng 居喪 91.33

kǎi 鎧 136.2
kǎi 豈 290
kān 堪 16.2
kāngníng 康寧 139
kě 可 118
kě yǐ 可以 50
kěduó 可奪 288
kǒngjí 恐急 176
kòu 叩 6
kòutóu 叩頭 6
kuāng 匡 288
kuángyán 狂言 172
kuānrén 寬仁 183
kūlìn 哭臨 91.38
kūn 昆 126
kūndì 昆弟 126

lài 賴 197
làn 爛 209
láng 郎 7
lángguān 郎官 93
lángpúyè 郎僕射 22
láo 牢 89
lègōng 勒功 291
lěi 累 136.4
Lèlíng 樂陵 199
Lèpíng 樂平 137
lǐ 里 1, 120
lì 吏 2
Lǐ Qí 李奇 147.2
Lì wáng 厲王 107.3
liàn 斂 136.6
liǎn 斂 136.6
liáng 梁 63.2
liáng 涼 136.7
liángrén 良人 101.1
liánmíng 連名 72
liǎnróng 斂容 128
liántǐ 連體 126
liánzhèng 廉正 175
liánzhuì 連綴 136.2
liánzuò 連坐 194
lièhóu 列侯 57
liètǔ 裂土 210
lìmín 吏民 152
lín 鄰 206
lín, lìn 臨 86
lǐng 領 125
lìng 令 29
lǐng Hú Yuè jì 領胡越騎 161
lǐng shàngshū shì 領尚書事 137, 152
línglièchē 軨獵車 120
línwèn 臨問 129
lísàn 離散 177
liǔ 柳 136.7
Liú Kuí 劉逵 91.43
Liú Qūlí 劉屈氂 101.2
liǔshà 柳翣 136.7
lǐxià 禮下 128
lǐyì 禮誼 80
lìyì 立意 201.3
lìyì 立議 63.3
lìzú 吏卒 216
lòu 漏 91.35
lǚ 縷 136.2
lù 錄 18
luán 鸞 89
luánqí 鸞旗 89
lüè 略 83
lùn 論 157

máng 芒 213
mǎng 莽 17
mángcì 芒刺 213
mángcì zài bèi 芒刺在背 213
máo 旄 93
Màolíng 茂陵 135
màoshèng 茂盛 139
méimù 眉目 21
mèisǐ 昧死 79
mèixù 妹壻 197
méng 蒙 211
Mèng Kāng 孟康 38.2
miǎn 免 40
miǎnfàng 免放 101.1
miǎnguān 免冠 40
miànmù 面目 60
miǎnnú 免奴 93
miàocí 廟祠 97
miàotáng 廟堂 287
miáoyì 苗裔 290
mìbì 密閉 136.7
míhuò 迷惑 100
míng 明 24
míng'ēn 明恩 122
mìshū 祕書 192
mò 莫 146
mò 嘿 206
mò 默 169
mòrán 默然 169
mòshòu 墨綬 93
móu 牟 88
Móushǒu 牟首 88
mù 沐 27
mù 暮 85
mùfǔ 莫府 36
mùyuán 墓園 147.2

nà 內 27
nǎizhě 乃者 195
nán 難 184.3
nán 男 12
nánzǐ 男子 181
nèi 內 16.6, 27
nèishì 內侍 286
nèixíng 內行 28
néng 能 107.5
nì 逆 17
niǎn 輦 65
niǎndào 輦道 88

zhà 詐 34
zhāi 齋 120
zhái 宅 6, 188
zhài 責 20.6
zhǎn 斬 61
zhàn 湛 94
zhǎncuī 斬縗 82
zhǎng 長 60, 136
zhàng 丈 136.4
zhǎng gōngzhǔ 長公主 28
zhǎngē 斬割 91.32
zhǎngshǐ 長史 36
zhāngwéi 張圍 146
zhǎngzhǔ 長主 30
zhànnì 湛溺 288
zhāo 朝 12
zhào 召 23
zhào 詔 24
Zhāo-hòu 昭后 32.1
zhàojiàn 召見 29
Zhāolíng 昭靈 143
zhāomù 朝暮 85
Zhāotái gōng 昭臺宮 193
zhàoyù 詔獄 68
zhé 輒 27
zhèn 震 46
zhèn 陳 64
zhèn 酖 20
zhēng 徵 82
zhèng 正 189
Zhèng shì 鄭氏 91.43
zhèngchén 爭臣 108
zhēngdào 爭道 150
zhēngfā 徵發 98
Zhēnghé 征和 10
zhènglìng 政令 114.4
zhēngshù 蒸庶 139
zhérù 輒入 27
zhī 知 151
zhí 直 91.32
zhí 執 38
zhì 秩 24
zhì 彘 90
zhì 制 142
zhì 治 143
zhì 識 22
zhìdù 制度 100
zhìjīn 至今 118
zhíjīnwú 執金吾 76
zhírèn 職任 16.3
zhítū 直突 205
zhítuì 執退 38
zhīyōu 知憂 151
zhīzǐ 支子 117
zhǒng 冢 91.42
zhòng 眾 88
zhòng èrqiān shí 中二千石 57
zhōng yùfǔ 中御府 86
zhōngchén 中臣 68
zhōngchén 忠臣 44
zhōnggōng 中宮 31
zhōnghuángmén 中黃門 65
zhōngláng 中郎 52
zhōngláng jiàng 中郎將 52
zhōngmíng 中明 136.4
zhòngshèn 重慎 91.35
zhòngshù 眾庶 24
zhōngshū lìng 中 悀 令 174
zhōngxìn 忠信 291
zhǒngyuán 冢園 147.2
zhōngzhèng 忠正 122
zhōu 調 36
Zhōu gōng 周公 12
Zhōu Xiāng wáng 周襄王 104
zhū 珠 133
zhū 誅 17
zhǔ 屬 11
zhù 著 43.2
zhuàng 狀 64
zhuàngdà 壯大 3
zhuānquán 專權 36
zhuànshè 傳舍 4
zhuānzhì 專制 31
zhūcáo dàfū 諸曹大夫 126
zhūcáo shìzhōng 諸曹侍中 7
zhūfá 誅罰 178
zhūhóu 諸侯 12
zhūlì 諸吏 78
zhūmiè 誅滅 194
zhuó 著 43.2
zhuó 擢 51
zhuólàn 灼爛 206
zhǔrén 主人 205
zhūshā 誅殺 114
zhùshí 柱石 54
zhūyí 誅夷 290
zǐ 子 12, 106
zǐ 姊 3
zì 自 3
zì jué yú tiān 自絕於天 111
zìài 自愛 112
zìān 自安 49
zìcái 自裁 68
zǐdì 子弟 34
zǐfū 姊夫 97
zǐgōng 梓宮 133
zǐmèi 姊妹 197
zǐnán 子男 19
zìruò 自若 152
zìshā 自殺 46
zìxīn 自新 196
zìxǐng 自省 169.3
zīxìng 資性 22
zǐxù 姊婿 158

漢書・霍光傳

漢書卷六十八

霍光金日磾傳第三十八

霍光字子孟，票騎將軍去病弟也。父中孺，河東平陽人也，〔一〕以縣吏給事平陽侯家，〔二〕與侍者衞少兒私通而生去病。中孺吏畢歸家，娶婦生光，因絕不相聞。久之，少兒女弟子夫得幸於武帝，立爲皇后，去病以皇后姊子貴幸。既壯大，乃自知父爲霍中孺，未及求問。會爲票騎將軍擊匈奴，道出河東，河東太守郊迎，負弩矢先驅，〔三〕至平陽傳舍，遣吏迎霍中孺。中孺趨入拜謁，將軍迎拜，因跪曰：「去病不早自知爲大人遺體也。」中孺扶服叩頭，〔四〕曰：「老臣得託命將軍，此天力也。」去病大爲中孺買田宅奴婢而去。還，復過焉，乃將光西至長安，時年十餘歲，任光爲郎，稍遷諸曹侍中。去病死後，光爲奉（常）〔車〕都尉光祿大夫，出則奉車，入侍左右，出入禁闥二十餘年，〔五〕小心謹慎，未嘗有過，甚見親信。

〔一〕師古曰：「中讀曰仲。」

〔二〕師古曰：「縣遣吏於侯家供事也。」
〔三〕師古曰：「郊迎，迎於郊界之上也。先驅者，導其路也。」
〔四〕師古曰：「服音蒲北反。」
〔五〕師古曰：「宮中小門謂之闥。」

征和二年，衞太子爲江充所敗，而燕王旦、廣陵王胥皆多過失。是時上年老，寵姬鉤弋趙倢伃有男，〔一〕上心欲以爲嗣，命大臣輔之。察羣臣唯光任大重，可屬社稷。〔二〕上乃使黃門畫者畫周公負成王朝諸侯以賜光。〔三〕後元二年春，上游五柞宮，病篤，光涕泣問曰：「如有不諱，誰當嗣者？」〔四〕上曰：「君未諭前畫意邪？〔五〕立少子，君行周公之事。」光頓首讓曰：「臣不如金日磾。」日磾亦曰：「臣外國人，不如光。」上以光爲大司馬大將軍，日磾爲車騎將軍，及太僕上官桀爲左將軍，搜粟都尉桑弘羊爲御史大夫，皆拜臥內牀下，〔六〕受遺詔輔少主。明日，武帝崩，太子襲尊號，是爲孝昭皇帝。帝年八歲，政事壹決於光。

〔一〕師古曰：「倢伃居鉤弋宮，故稱之。」
〔二〕師古曰：「任，堪也。屬，委也。任音壬。屬音之欲反。」
〔三〕師古曰：「黃門之署，職任親近，以供天子，百物在焉，故亦有畫工。」
〔四〕師古曰：「不諱，言不可諱也。」
〔五〕師古曰：「諭，曉也。」

〔六〕師古曰：「於天子所臥牀前拜職。」

先是，後元年，侍中僕射莽何羅與弟重合侯通謀爲逆，〔一〕時光與金日磾、上官桀等共誅之，功未錄。武帝病，封璽書曰：「帝崩發書以從事。」遺詔封金日磾爲秺侯，上官桀爲安陽侯，光爲博陸侯，〔二〕皆以前捕反者功封。時衞尉王莽子男忽侍中，〔三〕揚語曰：〔四〕「帝（病）〔崩〕，忽常在左右，安得遺詔封三子事！〔五〕羣兒自相貴耳。」光聞之，切讓王莽，〔六〕莽酖殺忽。

〔一〕師古曰：「莽音莫戶反。」

〔二〕文穎曰：「博，大。陸，平。取其嘉名，無此縣也，食邑北海、河（間）〔閒〕、東（城）〔郡〕。」師古曰：「蓋亦取鄉聚之名以爲國號，非必縣也，公孫弘平津鄉則是矣。」

〔三〕師古曰：「即右將軍王莽也，其子名忽。」

〔四〕師古曰：「揚謂宣唱之。」

〔五〕師古曰：「安猶焉。」

〔六〕師古曰：「切，深也。讓，責也。」

光爲人沈靜詳審，長財七尺三寸，〔一〕白晳，疏眉目，美須頿。〔二〕每出入下殿門，止進有常處，郎僕射竊識視之，不失尺寸，〔三〕其資性端正如此。初輔幼主，政自己出，〔四〕天下想聞其風采。〔五〕殿中嘗有怪，一夜羣臣相驚，光召尚符璽郎，〔六〕郎不肯授光。光欲奪之，郎按劍曰：「臣頭可得，璽不可得也！」光甚誼之。明日，詔增此郎秩二等。衆庶莫不多

25 光。〔七〕

〔一〕師古曰：「財與纔同。」

〔二〕師古曰：「晳，潔白也。髯，頰毛也。晳音先歷反。髯音人占反。」

〔三〕師古曰：「識，記也，音式志反。」

〔四〕師古曰：「自，從也。」

〔五〕師古曰：「采，文采。」

〔六〕師古曰：「恐有變難，故欲收(其)〔取〕璽。」

〔七〕師古曰：「多猶重也。以此事爲多足重也。」

26 光與左將軍桀結婚相親，光長女爲桀子安妻。有女年與帝相配，〔一〕桀因帝姊鄂邑蓋主
27 內安女後宮爲倢伃，〔二〕數月立爲皇后。父安爲票騎將軍，封桑樂侯。光時休沐出，桀輒入
28 代光決事。桀父子既尊盛，而德長公主。〔三〕公主內行不修，近幸河間丁外人。桀、安欲爲外
29 人求封，幸依國家故事以列侯尚公主者，光不許。又爲外人求光祿大夫，欲令得召見，又不
30 許。長主大以是怨光。而桀、安數爲外人求官爵弗能得，亦慙。自先帝時，桀已爲九卿，位
31 在光右。〔四〕及父子並爲將軍，有椒房中宮之重，〔五〕皇后親安女，光乃其外祖，而顧專制朝
32 事，〔六〕繇是與光爭權。〔七〕

〔一〕晉灼曰：「漢語光嫡妻東閭氏生安夫人，昭后之母也。」

〔二〕師古曰：「鄂邑，所食邑，爲蓋侯所尙，故云蓋主也。」
〔三〕師古曰：「懷其恩德也。」
〔四〕師古曰：「右，上也。」
〔五〕師古曰：「椒房殿，皇后所居。」
〔六〕師古曰：「顧猶反也。」
〔七〕師古曰：「繇讀與由同。」

燕王旦自以昭帝兄，常懷怨望。及御史大夫桑弘羊建造酒榷鹽鐵，爲國興利，伐其功，〔一〕欲爲子弟得官，亦怨恨光。於是蓋主、上官桀、安及弘羊皆與燕王旦通謀，詐令人爲燕王上書，言「光出都肄郎羽林，道上稱蹕，〔二〕太官先置。〔三〕又引蘇武前使匈奴，拘留二十年不降，還乃爲典屬國，而大將軍長史敞亡功爲搜粟都尉。〔四〕又擅調益莫府校尉。〔五〕光專權自恣，疑有非常。臣旦願歸符璽，入宿衞，察姦臣變。」候司光出沐日奏之。桀欲從中下其事，〔六〕桑弘羊當與諸大臣共執退光。書奏，帝不肯下。

〔一〕師古曰：「伐，矜也。」
〔二〕孟康曰：「都，試也。肄，習也。」師古曰：「謂總閱試習武備也。」
〔三〕師古曰：「供飲食之具。」
〔四〕師古曰：「楊敞也。」

〔五〕師古曰：「調，選也。莫府，大將軍府也。調音徒釣反。」

〔六〕師古曰：「下謂下有司也，音胡稼反。」

明日，光聞之，止畫室中不入。〔一〕上問「大將軍安在？」左將軍桀對曰：「以燕王告其罪，故不敢入。」有詔召大將軍。光入，免冠頓首謝，上曰：「將軍冠。〔二〕朕知是書詐也，將軍亡罪。」光曰：「陛下何以知之？」上曰：「將軍之廣明，都郎屬耳。〔三〕調校尉以來未能十日，燕王何以得知之？且將軍爲非，不須校尉。」〔四〕是時帝年十四，尚書左右皆驚，而上書者果亡，捕之甚急。桀等懼，白上小事不足遂，〔五〕上不聽。

〔一〕如淳曰：「近臣所止計畫之室也，或曰彫畫之室。」師古曰：「彫畫是也。」

〔二〕師古曰：「令復著冠也。」

〔三〕師古曰：「之，往也。廣明，亭名也。屬耳，近耳也。屬音之欲反。」

〔四〕文穎曰：「帝云將軍欲反，不由一校尉。」

〔五〕師古曰：「遂猶竟也。不須窮竟也。」

後桀黨與有譖光者，上輒怒曰：「大將軍忠臣，先帝所屬以輔朕身，〔一〕敢有毀者坐之。」自是桀等不敢復言，乃謀令長公主置酒請光，伏兵格殺之，因廢帝，迎立燕王爲天子。事發覺，光盡誅桀、安、弘羊、外人宗族。燕王、蓋主皆自殺。光威震海內。昭帝既冠，遂委任光，訖十三年，百姓充實，四夷賓服。

〔一〕師古曰：「屬，委也，音之欲反。其下亦同。」

元平元年，昭帝崩，亡嗣。武帝六男獨有廣陵王胥在，羣臣議所立，咸持廣陵王。王本以行失道，先帝所不用。光內不自安。郎有上書言「周太王廢太伯立王季，文王舍伯邑考立武王，唯在所宜，〔一〕雖廢長立少可也。廣陵王不可以承宗廟。」言合光意。光以其書視丞相敞等，〔二〕擢郎爲九江太守，即日承皇太后詔，遣行大鴻臚事少府樂成、宗正德、光祿大夫吉、中郎將利漢迎昌邑王賀。

〔一〕師古曰：「太伯者，王季之兄。伯邑考，文王長子也。」

〔二〕師古曰：「視讀曰示。敞即楊敞也。」

賀者，武帝孫，昌邑哀王子也。既至，即位，行淫亂。光憂懣，〔一〕獨以問所親故吏大司農田延年。延年曰：「將軍爲國柱石，〔二〕審此人不可，何不建白太后，〔三〕更選賢而立之？」光曰：「今欲如是，於古嘗有此否？」〔四〕延年曰：「伊尹相殷，廢太甲以安宗廟，後世稱其忠。〔五〕將軍若能行此，亦漢之伊尹也。」光乃引延年給事中，陰與車騎將軍張安世圖計，〔六〕遂召丞相、御史、將軍、列侯、中二千石、大夫、博士會議未央宮。光曰：「昌邑王行昏亂，恐危社稷，如何？」羣臣皆驚鄂失色，〔七〕莫敢發言，但唯唯而已。田延年前，離席按劍，曰：「先帝屬將軍以幼孤，寄將軍以天下，以將軍忠賢能安劉氏也。今羣下鼎沸，社稷將傾，且

漢之傳諡常爲孝者，以長有天下，令宗廟血食也。如令漢家絕祀，〔八〕將軍雖死，何面目見先帝於地下乎？今日之議，不得旋踵。〔九〕羣臣後應者，臣請劍斬之。」光謝曰：「九卿責光是也。天下匈匈不安，光當受難。」〔一〇〕於是議者皆叩頭，曰：「萬姓之命在於將軍，唯大將軍令。」〔一一〕

〔一〕師古曰：「懣音滿，又音悶。」

〔二〕師古曰：「柱者，梁下之柱；石者，承柱之礎也。言大臣負國重任，如屋之柱及其石也。」

〔三〕師古曰：「立議而白之。」

〔四〕師古曰：「光不涉學，故有此問也。」

〔五〕師古曰：「商書太甲篇曰『太甲既立，弗明，伊尹放諸桐』是也。」

〔六〕師古曰：「圖，謀也。」

〔七〕師古曰：「凡言鄂者，皆謂阻礙不依順也，後字作愕，其義亦同。」

〔八〕師古曰：「如，若也。」

〔九〕師古曰：「宜速決。」

〔一〇〕師古曰：「受其憂責也。」

〔一一〕師古曰：「言一聽之也。」

光即與羣臣俱見白太后，具陳昌邑王不可以承宗廟狀。皇太后乃車駕幸未央承明殿，

詔諸禁門毋內昌邑羣臣。王入朝太后還，乘輦欲歸溫室，中黃門宦者各持門扇，王入，門閉，昌邑羣臣不得入。王曰：「何爲？」大將軍跪曰：「有皇太后詔，毋內昌邑羣臣。」王曰：「徐之，何乃驚人如是！」光使盡驅出昌邑羣臣，置金馬門外。車騎將軍安世將羽林騎收縛二百餘人，皆送廷尉詔獄。令故昭帝侍中中臣侍守王。光敕左右：「謹宿衛，卒有物故自裁，令我負天下，有殺主名。」〔一〕王尚未自知當廢，謂左右：「我故羣臣從官安得罪，而大將軍盡繫之乎。」〔二〕頃之，有太后詔召王。王聞召，意恐，乃曰：「我安得罪而召我哉！」太后被珠襦，〔三〕盛服坐武帳中，侍御數百人皆持兵，期門武士陛戟，陳列殿下。〔四〕羣臣以次上殿，召昌邑王伏前聽詔。光與羣臣連名奏王，尚書令讀奏曰：

〔一〕師古曰：「卒讀曰猝。物故，死也。自裁，自殺也。」

〔二〕師古曰：「安，焉也。」

〔三〕如淳曰：「以珠飾襦也。」晉灼曰：「貫珠以爲襦，形若今革襦矣。」師古曰：「晉說是也。」

〔四〕師古曰：「陛戟謂執戟以衞陛下也。」

丞相臣敞、〔一〕大司馬大將軍臣光、車騎將軍臣安世、〔二〕度遼將軍臣明友、〔三〕前將軍臣增、〔四〕後將軍臣充國、〔五〕御史大夫臣誼、〔六〕宜春侯臣譚、〔七〕當塗侯臣聖、〔八〕隨桃侯臣昌樂、〔九〕杜侯臣屠耆堂、〔一〇〕太僕臣延年、〔一一〕太常臣昌、〔一二〕大司農臣延

年、〔二三〕宗正臣德、〔二四〕少府臣樂成、〔二五〕廷尉臣光、〔二六〕執金吾臣延壽、〔二七〕大鴻臚臣賢、〔二八〕左馮翊臣廣明、〔二九〕右扶風臣德、〔三〇〕長信少府臣嘉、〔三一〕典屬國臣武、〔三二〕京輔都尉臣廣漢、〔三三〕司隸校尉臣辟兵、〔三四〕諸吏文學光祿大夫臣遷、〔三五〕臣畸、〔三六〕臣吉、〔三七〕臣賜、臣管、臣勝、臣梁、臣長幸、〔三八〕臣夏侯勝、〔三九〕太中大夫臣德、〔四〇〕臣卬〔四一〕昧死言皇太后陛下：臣敞等頓首死罪。(大)〔天〕子所以永保宗廟總壹海內者，以慈孝禮誼賞罰爲本。孝昭皇帝早棄天下，亡嗣，臣敞等議，禮曰「爲人後者爲之子也」，昌邑王宜嗣後，遣宗正、大鴻臚、光祿大夫奉節使徵昌邑王典喪。服斬縗，〔四二〕亡悲哀之心，廢禮誼，居道上不素食，〔四三〕使從官略女子載衣車，內所居傳舍。始至謁見，立爲皇太子，常私買雞豚以食。受皇帝信璽、行璽大行前，〔四四〕就次發璽不封。〔四五〕從官更持節，〔四六〕引內昌邑從官騶宰官奴二百餘人，常與居禁闥內敖戲。自之符璽取節十六，〔四七〕朝暮臨，〔四八〕令從官更持節從。〔四九〕爲書曰「皇帝問侍中君卿：〔五〇〕使中御府令高昌奉黃金千斤，賜君卿取十妻。」大行在前殿，發樂府樂器，引內昌邑樂人，擊鼓歌吹作俳倡。〔五一〕會下還，上前殿，〔五二〕擊鐘磬，召內泰壹宗廟樂人輦道牟首，〔五三〕鼓吹歌舞，悉奏衆樂。發長安廚三太牢具祠閣室中，〔五四〕祀已，與從官飲啗。〔五五〕駕法駕，皮軒鸞旗，驅馳北宮、桂宮，弄彘鬬虎。〔五六〕召皇太后御小馬車，〔五七〕使官奴騎乘，遊戲掖庭中。與孝昭皇帝宮人

蒙等淫亂，詔掖庭令敢泄言要斬。

〔一〕師古曰：「楊敞也。」
〔二〕師古曰：「張子孺。」
〔三〕師古曰：「范明友。」
〔四〕師古曰：「韓增。」
〔五〕師古曰：「趙充國。」
〔六〕師古曰：「蔡誼。」
〔七〕師古曰：「王訢子。」
〔八〕師古曰：「姓魏也。」
〔九〕師古曰：「姓趙，故蒼梧王趙光子。」
〔一〇〕師古曰：「故胡人。」
〔一一〕師古曰：「杜延年。」
〔一二〕師古曰：「蒲侯蘇昌。」
〔一三〕師古曰：「田延年。」
〔一四〕師古曰：「劉向父。」
〔一五〕師古曰：「姓史也。」
〔一六〕師古曰：「李光。」

〔一七〕師古曰：「李延壽。」

〔一八〕師古曰：「韋賢。」

〔一九〕師古曰：「田廣明。」

〔二〇〕師古曰：「周德。」

〔二一〕師古曰：「不知姓。」

〔二二〕師古曰：「蘇武。」

〔二三〕師古曰：「趙廣漢。」

〔二四〕師古曰：「不知姓。」

〔二五〕師古曰：「王遷。」

〔二六〕師古曰：「宋畸。」

〔二七〕師古曰：「景吉。」

〔二八〕師古曰：「並不知姓也。」

〔二九〕李奇曰：「同官同名，故以姓別也。」

〔三〇〕師古曰：「不知姓。」

〔三一〕師古曰：「趙充國子也。」

〔三二〕師古曰：「典喪服，嘗爲喪主也。斬縗，謂縗裳下不緶，直斬（斬）割之而已。緶音步千反。」

〔三三〕師古曰：「素食，菜食無肉也。言王在道常肉食，非居喪之制也。而鄭康成解喪服素食云『平常之食』，失之遠矣。」

素食，義亦見王莽傳。」

〔三四〕孟康曰：「漢初有三璽，天子之璽自佩，行璽、信璽在符節臺。大行前，昭帝柩前也。」韋昭曰：「大行，不反之辭也。」

〔三五〕師古曰：「璽既國器，常當緘封，而王於大行前受之，退還所次，遂爾發漏，更不封之，得令凡人皆見，言不重慎也。」

〔三六〕師古曰：「更音工衡反。次下亦同。」

〔三七〕師古曰：「之，往也。自往至署取節也。」

〔三八〕師古曰：「臨，哭臨也，音力禁反。」

〔三九〕師古曰：「更互執節，從至哭臨之所。」

〔四〇〕師古曰：「昌邑之侍中名君卿也。」

〔四一〕師古曰：「俳優，諧戲也。倡，樂人也。俳音排。」

〔四二〕如淳曰：「下謂柩之入冢。葬還不居喪位，便處前殿也。」師古曰：「下音胡稼反。」

〔四三〕鄭氏曰：「祭泰壹神樂人也。」孟康曰：「牟首，地名也，上有觀。」如淳曰：「輦道，閣道也。牟首，屏面也。以屏面自隔，無哀戚也。」臣瓚曰：「牟首，池名也，在上林苑中。方在衰絰而輦游於池，言無哀戚也。」師古曰：「召泰壹樂人，內之於輦道牟首而鼓吹歌舞也。牟首，瓚說是也。屏面之言，失之遠矣。又左思吳都賦云『長塗牟首』，劉逵以爲牟首閣道有室屋也，此說更無所出。或者思及逵據此『輦道牟首』便誤用之乎？」

〔四四〕如淳曰：「黃圖北出中門有長安廚，故謂之廚城門。閣室，閣道之有室者。不知禱何淫祀也。」

〔四五〕師古曰：「哈，食也，音徒敢反。」

〔四六〕師古曰：「皮軒鸞旗皆法駕所陳也。北宮、桂宮並在未央宮北。」

〔四七〕張晏曰：「皇太后所駕遊宮中輦車也。漢廄有果下馬，高三尺，以駕輦。」師古曰：「小馬可於果樹下乘之，故號果下馬。」

太后曰：「止！〔一〕為人臣子當悖亂如是邪！」〔二〕王離席伏。尚書令復讀曰：

〔一〕師古曰：「令且止讀奏。」

〔二〕師古曰：「責王也。悖，乖也，音布內反。」

取諸侯王列侯二千石綬及墨綬黃綬以并佩昌邑郎官者免奴。〔一〕變易節上黃旄以赤。〔二〕發御府金錢刀劍玉器采繒，賞賜所與遊戲者。與從官官奴夜飲，湛沔於酒。〔三〕詔太官上乘輿食如故。食監奏未釋服未可御故食，〔四〕復詔太官趣具，無關食監。〔五〕太官不敢具，即使從官出買雞豚，詔殿門內，以為常。〔六〕獨夜設九賓溫室，〔七〕延見姊夫昌邑關內侯。祖宗廟祠未舉，為璽書使使者持節，以三太牢祠昌邑哀王園廟，稱嗣子皇帝。〔八〕受璽以來二十七日，使者旁午，〔九〕持節詔諸官署徵發，凡千一百二十七事。文學光祿大夫夏侯勝等及侍中傅嘉數進諫以過失，使人簿責勝，〔一〇〕縛嘉繫獄。荒淫迷惑，失帝王禮誼，亂漢制度。臣敞等數進諫，不變更，〔一一〕日以益甚，恐危社稷，

天下不安。

〔一〕師古曰：「免奴謂免放爲良人者。」
〔二〕師古曰：「以劉屈氂與戾太子戰，加節上黃旄，遂以爲常。賀今輒改之。」
〔三〕師古曰：「湛讀曰沈，又讀曰躭。沈沔，荒迷也。」
〔四〕師古曰：「釋謂解脫也。」
〔五〕師古曰：「趣讀曰促。關，由也。」
〔六〕師古曰：「內，入也。令每日常入雞豚也。」
〔七〕師古曰：「於溫室中設九賓之禮也。九賓，解在叔孫通傳。」
〔八〕師古曰：「時在喪服，故未祠宗廟而私祭昌邑哀王也。」
〔九〕如淳曰：「旁午，分布也。」師古曰：「一從一橫爲旁午，猶言交橫也。」
〔一〇〕師古曰：「簿音步戶反。簿責，以文簿具責之。」
〔一一〕師古曰：「更，改也。」

臣敞等謹與博士臣霸、臣雋舍、〔一〕臣德、臣虞舍、臣射、臣倉議，皆曰：「高皇帝建功業爲漢太祖，孝文皇帝慈仁節儉爲太宗，今陛下嗣孝昭皇帝後，行淫辟不軌。〔二〕詩云：『籍曰未知，亦既抱子。』〔三〕五辟之屬，莫大不孝。〔四〕周襄王不能事母，春秋曰『天王出居于鄭』，繇不孝出之，絕之於天下也。〔五〕宗廟重於君，陛下未見命高廟，不可以

承天序，奉祖宗廟，子萬姓，當廢。」臣請有司御史大夫臣誼、宗正臣德、太常臣昌與太祝以一太牢具，告祠高廟。臣敞等昧死以聞。

〔一〕晉灼曰：「嶲姓，舍名也。下有臣虞舍，故以姓別之。」師古曰：「嶲音辭阮反，又音字阮反。」

〔二〕師古曰：「軌，法也。辟讀曰僻。」

〔三〕師古曰：「大雅抑之詩。衞武公刺厲王也。籍，假也。此言假令人云王尚幼少，未有所知，亦已長大而抱子矣，實不幼少也。」

〔四〕師古曰：「五辟即五刑也。辟音頻亦反。」

〔五〕師古曰：「襄王，惠王子也。僖二十四年經書『天王出居于鄭』。公羊傳曰：『王者無外，此其言出何？不能乎母也。』繇讀與由同。」

皇太后詔曰：「可。」光令王起拜受詔，王曰：「聞天子有爭臣七人，雖無道不失天下。」〔一〕光曰：「皇太后詔廢，安得天子！」乃卽持其手，〔二〕解脫其璽組，奉上太后，扶王下殿，出金馬門，羣臣隨送。王西面拜，曰：「愚戇不任漢事。」起就乘輿副車。大將軍光送至昌邑邸，光謝曰：「王行自絕於天，臣等駑怯，不能殺身報德。臣寧負王，不敢負社稷。願王自愛，臣長不復見左右。」〔三〕光涕泣而去。羣臣奏言：「古者廢放之人屏於遠方，不及以政，〔四〕請徙王賀漢中房陵縣。」太后詔歸賀昌邑，賜湯沐邑二千戶。昌邑羣臣坐亡輔導之誼，陷王於惡，光悉誅殺二百餘人。出死，號呼市中〔五〕曰：「當斷不斷，反受其亂。」〔六〕

〔一〕師古曰：「引孝經之言。」

〔二〕師古曰：「即，就也。」

〔三〕師古曰：「言不復得侍見於左右。」

〔四〕師古曰：「言不豫政令。」

〔五〕師古曰：「呼音火故反。」

〔六〕師古曰：「悔不早殺光等也。」

光坐庭中，會丞相以下議定所立。廣陵王已前不用，及燕刺王反誅，其子不在議中。近親唯有衛太子孫號皇曾孫在民間，咸稱述焉。光遂復與丞相敞等上奏曰：「禮曰『人道親親故尊祖，尊祖故敬宗。』(太)〔大〕宗亡嗣，擇支子孫賢者爲嗣。孝武皇帝曾孫病已，武帝時有詔掖庭養視，至今年十八，師受詩、論語、孝經，躬行節儉，慈仁愛人，可以嗣孝昭皇帝後，奉承祖宗廟，子萬姓。臣昧死以聞。」皇太后詔曰：「可。」光遣宗正劉德至曾孫家尚冠里，洗沐賜御衣，太僕以軨獵車迎曾孫就齋宗正府，入未央宮見皇太后，封爲陽武侯。〔一〕已而光奉上皇帝璽綬，謁于高廟，是爲孝宣皇帝。明年，下詔曰：「夫褒有德，賞元功，古今通誼也。大司馬大將軍光宿衛忠正，宣德明恩，守節秉誼，以安宗廟。其以河北、東武陽益封光萬七千戶。」與故所食凡二萬戶。賞賜前後黃金七千斤，錢六千萬，雜繒三萬疋，奴婢百

七十人，馬二千疋，甲第一區。

〔一〕師古曰：「解並在宣紀。軨音零。」

自昭帝時，光子禹及兄孫雲皆中郎將，雲弟山奉車都尉侍中，領胡越兵。光兩女壻爲東西宮衞尉，昆弟諸壻外孫皆奉朝請，爲諸曹大夫，騎都尉，給事中。黨親連體，根據於朝廷。光自後元秉持萬機，及上即位，乃歸政。上謙讓不受，諸事皆先關白光，然後奏御天子。光每朝見，上虛己斂容，禮下之已甚。〔一〕

〔一〕師古曰：「下音胡稼反。」

光秉政前後二十年，地節二年春病篤，車駕自臨問光病，上爲之涕泣。光上書謝恩曰：「願分國邑三千戶，以封兄孫奉車都尉山爲列侯，奉兄票騎將軍去病祀。」事下丞相御史，即日拜光子禹爲右將軍。

光薨，上及皇太后親臨光喪。太中大夫任宣與侍御史五人持節護喪事。中二千石治莫府冢上。〔一〕賜金錢、繒絮，繡被百領，衣五十篋，璧珠璣玉衣，〔二〕梓宮、〔三〕便房、黃腸題湊各一具，〔四〕樅木外臧椁十五具。〔五〕東園溫明，〔六〕皆如乘輿制度。載光尸柩以轀輬車，〔七〕黃屋左纛，〔八〕發材官輕車北軍五校士軍陳至茂陵，以送其葬。謚曰宣成侯。發三河卒穿復土，起冢祠堂，置園邑三百家，長丞奉守如舊法。

〔一〕如淳曰：「典爲冢者。」

〔二〕師古曰：「漢儀注以玉爲襦，如鎧狀連綴之，以黃金爲縷，要已下玉爲札，長尺，廣二寸半爲甲，下至足，亦綴以黃金縷。」

〔三〕服虔曰：「棺也。」師古曰：「以梓木爲之，親身之棺也。爲天子制，故亦稱梓宮。」

〔四〕服虔曰：「便房，藏中便坐也。」蘇林曰：「以柏木黃心致累棺外，故曰黃腸。木頭皆內向，故曰題湊。」如淳曰：「漢儀注天子陵中明中高丈二尺四寸，周二丈，內梓宮，次楩椁，柏黃腸題湊。」師古曰：「便房，小曲室也。如氏以爲楩木名，非也。」

〔五〕服虔曰：「在正臧外，婢妾臧也。或曰廚廄之屬也。」蘇林曰：「樅木，柏葉松身。」師古曰：「爾雅及毛詩傳並云樅木松葉柏身，檜木乃柏葉松身耳。蘇說非也。樅音七庸反。檜音工闊反，字亦作栝。」

〔六〕服虔曰：「東園處此器，形如方漆桶，開一面，漆畫之，以鏡置其中，以懸屍上，大斂幷蓋之。」師古曰：「東園，署名也，屬少府。其署主作此器也。」

〔七〕文穎曰：「轀輬車，如今喪轜車也。」孟康曰：「如衣車有窗牖，閉之則溫，開之則涼，故名之轀輬車也。」臣瓚曰：「秦始皇道崩，祕其事，載以轀輬車，百官奏事如故，此不得是轜車類也。案杜延年奏，載霍光柩以輬車，駕大廄白虎駟，以轀車駕大廄白鹿駟爲倅。」師古曰：「轀輬本安車也，可以臥息。後因載喪，飾以柳翣，故遂爲喪車耳。轀者密閉，輬者旁開窗牖，各別一乘，隨事爲名。後人既專以載喪，又去其一，總爲藩飾，而合二名呼之耳。倅，副也，音千內反。」

〔八〕師古曰：「解在高紀也。」

既葬，封山爲樂平侯，以奉車都尉領尚書事。天子思光功德，下詔曰：「故大司馬大將軍博陸侯宿衛孝武皇帝三十有餘年，輔孝昭皇帝十有餘年，遭大難，躬秉誼，率三公九卿大夫定萬世冊以安社稷，天下蒸庶咸以康寧。功德茂盛，朕甚嘉之。復其後世，疇其爵邑，〔一〕世世無有所與，功如蕭相國。」〔二〕明年夏，封太子外祖父許廣漢爲平恩侯。復下詔曰：「宣成侯光宿衛忠正，勤勞國家。善善及後世，〔三〕其封光兄孫中郎將雲爲冠陽侯。」

〔一〕應劭曰：「疇，等也。」師古曰：「復音方目反。」
〔二〕師古曰：「與讀曰豫。」
〔三〕師古曰：「善善者，謂褒寵善人也。」

禹既嗣爲博陸侯，太夫人顯改光時所自造塋制而侈大之。〔一〕起三出闕，築神道，北臨昭靈，南出承恩，〔二〕盛飾祠室，輦閣通屬永巷，而幽良人婢妾守之。〔三〕廣治第室，作乘輿輦，加畫繡絪馮，黃金塗，〔四〕韋絮薦輪，〔五〕侍婢以五采絲輓顯，游戲第中。〔六〕初，光愛幸監奴馮子都，常與計事，及顯寡居，與子都亂。〔七〕而禹、山亦並繕治第宅，走馬馳逐平樂館。雲當朝請，數稱病私出，〔八〕多從賓客，張圍獵黃山苑中，使蒼頭奴上朝謁，〔九〕莫敢譴者。而顯及諸女，晝夜出入長信宮殿中，亡期度。〔一〇〕

〔一〕師古曰：「塋，墓域也，音營。」

〔二〕服虔曰：「昭靈、承恩，皆館名也。」李奇曰：「昭靈，高祖母冢園也。」文穎曰：「承恩，宣平侯冢園也。」師古曰：「服說是也，文、李並失之。」

〔三〕晉灼曰：「閣道乃通屬至永巷中也。」師古曰：「此亦其冢上作輦閣之道及永巷也，非謂掖庭之永巷也。」

〔四〕如淳曰：「絪亦茵。馮（所謂）〔謂所〕馮者也，以黃金塗飾之。」師古曰：「茵，蓐也，以繡為茵馮而黃金塗輿輦也。」

〔五〕晉灼曰：「御輦以韋緣輪，著之以絮。」師古曰：「取其行安，不搖動也。著音張呂反。」

〔六〕師古曰：「輓謂牽引車輦也，音晚。」

〔七〕晉灼曰：「漢語東閭氏亡，顯以婢代立，素與馮殷姦也。」師古曰：「監奴，謂奴之監知家務者也，殷者，子都之名。」

〔八〕師古曰：「請音才姓反。」

〔九〕文穎曰：「朝當用謁，不自行而令奴上謁者也。」師古曰：「上謁，若今參見尊貴而通名也。」

〔一〇〕師古曰：「長信宮，上官太后所居。」

宣帝自在民間聞知霍氏尊盛日久，內不能善。光薨，上始躬親朝政，御史大夫魏相給事中。顯謂禹、雲、山：「女曹不務奉大將軍餘業，〔一〕今大夫給事中，他人壹間，女能復自救邪？」〔二〕後兩家奴爭道，〔三〕霍氏奴入御史府，欲躢大夫門，御史為叩頭謝，乃去。人以謂霍氏，〔四〕顯等始知憂。會魏大夫為丞相，數燕見言事。平恩侯與侍中金安上等徑出入省中。時霍山自若領尚書，〔五〕上令吏民得奏封事，不關尚書，羣臣進見獨往來，〔六〕於是霍氏甚惡之。

〔一〕師古曰：「女音汝。曹，輩也。」

〔二〕師古曰：「間音居莧反。」

〔三〕師古曰：「謂霍氏及御史家。」

〔四〕師古曰：「告語也。」

〔五〕師古曰：「自若猶言如故也。」

〔六〕師古曰：「謂各各得盡言於上也。」

宣帝始立，立微時許妃爲皇后。顯愛小女成君，欲貴之，私使乳醫淳于衍行毒藥殺許后，〔一〕因勸光內成君，代立爲后。語在外戚傳。始許后暴崩，吏捕諸醫，劾衍侍疾亡狀不道，下獄。吏簿問急，〔二〕顯恐事敗，即具以實語光。光大驚，欲自發舉，不忍，猶與。〔三〕會奏上，因署衍勿論。〔四〕光薨後，語稍泄。於是上始聞之而未察，〔五〕乃徙光女壻度遼將軍未央衞尉平陵侯范明友爲光祿勳，次壻諸吏中郎將羽林監任勝出爲安定太守。數月，復出光姊壻給事中光祿大夫張朔爲蜀郡太守，羣孫壻中郎將王漢爲武威太守。頃之，復徙光長女壻長樂衞尉鄧廣漢爲少府。更以禹爲大司馬，冠小冠，亡印綬，罷其右將軍屯兵官屬，特使禹官名與光俱大司馬者。〔六〕又收范明友度遼將軍印綬，但爲光祿勳。及光中女壻趙平爲散騎騎都尉光祿大夫將屯兵，又收平騎都尉印綬。諸領胡越騎、羽林及兩宮衞將屯兵，悉易

以所親信許、史子弟代之。

〔一〕師古曰：「乳醫，視產乳之疾者。乳音而樹反。」
〔二〕師古曰：「簿音步戶反。」
〔三〕師古曰：「猶與，不決也。與讀曰豫。」
〔四〕師古曰：「署者，題其奏後也。」
〔五〕師古曰：「未知其虛實。」
〔六〕蘇林曰：「特，但也。」

禹爲大司馬，稱病。禹故長史任宣候問，禹曰：「我何病？縣官非我家將軍不得至是，〔一〕今將軍墳墓未乾，盡外我家，〔二〕反任許、史，奪我印綬，令人不省死。」〔三〕宣見禹恨望深，〔四〕乃謂曰：「大將軍時何可復行！〔五〕持國權柄，殺生在手中。廷尉李种、王平、〔六〕左馮翊賈勝胡及車丞相女壻少府徐仁皆坐逆將軍（竟）〔意〕下獄死。使樂成小家子得幸將軍，至九卿封侯。〔七〕百官以下但事馮子都、王子方等，〔八〕視丞相亡如也。〔九〕各自有時，今許、史自天子骨肉，貴正宜耳。大司馬欲用是怨恨，愚以爲不可。」禹默然。數日，起視事。

〔一〕如淳曰：「縣官謂天子。」
〔二〕師古曰：「外謂疏斥之。」
〔三〕師古曰：「不自省有過也。」

〔四〕師古曰：「望，怨也。」

〔五〕師古曰：「言今何得復如此也。」

〔六〕師古曰：「种音沖。」

〔七〕師古曰：「即上所云少府樂成者也。使者，其姓也，字或作史。」

〔八〕服虔曰：「皆光奴。」

〔九〕師古曰：「亡如猶言無所象似也。」

顯及禹、山、雲自見日侵削，數相對啼泣，自怨。山曰：「今丞相用事，縣官信之，盡變易大將軍時法令，以公田賦與貧民，發揚大將軍過失。又諸儒生多窶人子，〔一〕遠客飢寒，喜妄說狂言，〔二〕不避忌諱，大將軍常讎之，〔三〕今陛下好與諸儒生語，人人自使書對事，多言我家者。嘗有上書言大將軍時主弱臣強，專制擅權，今其子孫用事，昆弟益驕恣，恐危宗廟，災異數見，盡爲是也。其言絕痛，山屛不奏其書。後上書者益黠，盡奏封事，輒（使）〔下〕中書令出取之，不關尚書，益不信人。」顯曰：「丞相數言我家，獨無罪乎？」山曰：「丞相廉正，安得罪？我家昆弟諸壻多不謹。又聞民間讙言霍氏毒殺許皇后，〔四〕寧有是邪？」顯恐急，即具以實告山、雲、禹。山、雲、禹驚曰：「如是，何不早告禹等！縣官離散斥逐諸壻，用是故也。此大事，誅罰不小，柰何？」於是始有邪謀矣。

〔一〕師古曰：「窶，貧而無禮，音其羽反。」

〔二〕師古曰：「喜音許吏反。」

〔三〕師古曰：「言嫉之如仇讎也。」

〔四〕師古曰：「讙，衆聲也，音（計）〔許〕爰反。」

初，趙平客石夏善為天官，〔一〕語平曰：「熒惑守御星，御星，太僕奉車都尉也，不黜則死。」平內憂山等。雲舅李竟所善張赦見雲家卒卒，〔二〕謂竟曰：「今丞相與平恩侯用事，可令太夫人言太后，先誅此兩人。移徙陛下，在太后耳。」長安男子張章告之，事下廷尉。執金吾捕張赦、石夏等，後有詔止勿捕。山等愈恐，相謂曰：「此縣官重太后，故不竟也。〔三〕然惡端已見，又有弒許后事，陛下雖寬仁，恐左右不聽，久之猶發，發即族矣，不如先也。」〔四〕遂令諸女各歸報其夫，皆曰：「安所相避？」〔五〕

〔一〕師古曰：「曉星文者。」

〔二〕師古曰：「卒讀曰猝，悤遽之貌也。」

〔三〕師古曰：「重，難也。竟，窮竟其事也。」

〔四〕師古曰：「言先反。」

〔五〕師古曰：「言無處相避，當受禍也。」

會李竟坐與諸侯王交通，辭語及霍氏，有詔雲、山不宜宿衛，免就第。光諸女遇太后無禮，〔一〕馮子都數犯法，上并以為讓，〔二〕山、禹等甚恐。顯夢第中井水溢流庭下，竈居樹上，

又夢大將軍謂顯曰：「知捕兒不？〔三〕亟下捕之。」〔四〕第中鼠暴多，與人相觸，以尾畫地。鴞數鳴殿前樹上。〔五〕第門自壞。雲尚冠里宅中門亦壞。巷端人共見有人居雲屋上，徹瓦投地，就視，亡有，大怪之。禹夢車騎聲正讙來捕禹，舉家憂愁。山曰：「丞相擅減宗廟羔、菟、鼃，〔六〕可以此罪也。」謀令太后爲博平君置酒，〔七〕召丞相、平恩侯以下，使范明友、鄧廣漢承太后制引斬之，因廢天子而立禹。約定未發，雲拜爲玄菟太守，太中大夫任宣爲代郡太守。山又坐寫祕書，顯爲上書獻城西第，入馬千匹，以贖山罪。書報聞。〔八〕會事發覺，雲、山、明友自殺，顯、禹、廣漢等捕得。禹要斬，顯及諸女昆弟皆棄市。唯獨霍后廢處昭臺宮。與霍氏相連坐誅滅者數千家。

〔一〕服虔曰：「光諸女自以（爲）〔於〕上官太后爲姨母，遇之無禮。」
〔二〕師古曰：「總以此事責之也。」
〔三〕師古曰：「知兒見捕否？」
〔四〕蘇林曰：「且疾下捕之。」師古曰：「亟音居力反。」
〔五〕師古曰：「鴞，惡聲之鳥也。古者室屋高大，則通呼爲殿耳，非止天子宮中。其語亦見黃霸傳。鴞音羽驕反。」
〔六〕如淳曰：「高后時定令，敢有擅議宗廟者，棄市。」師古曰：「羔、菟、鼃所以供祭也。」
〔七〕文穎曰：「宣帝外祖母也。」
〔八〕師古曰：「不許之。」

上乃下詔曰：「乃者東織室令史張赦使魏郡豪李竟報冠陽侯雲謀為大逆，〔一〕朕以大將軍故，抑而不揚，冀其自新。今大司馬博陸侯禹與母宣成侯夫人顯及從昆弟子冠陽侯雲、樂平侯山諸姊妹壻謀為大逆，欲詿誤百姓。賴(祖宗)〔宗廟〕神靈，先發得，咸伏其辜，〔二〕朕甚悼之。諸為霍氏所詿誤，事在丙申前，未發覺在吏者，皆赦除之。男子張章先發覺，以語期門董忠，忠告左曹楊惲，惲告侍中金安上。惲召見對狀，後章上書以聞。侍中史高與金安上建發其事，〔三〕言無入霍氏禁闥，卒不得遂其謀，〔四〕皆讎有功。〔五〕封章為博成侯，忠高昌侯，惲平通侯，安上都成侯，高樂陵侯。」

〔一〕師古曰：「解在宣紀也。」
〔二〕師古曰：「事發而捕得。」
〔三〕師古曰：「言共立意發之也。」
〔四〕師古曰：「遂，成也。」
〔五〕晉灼曰：「讎，等也。」師古曰：「言其功相等類也。」

初，霍氏奢侈，茂陵徐生曰：「霍氏必亡。夫奢則不遜，不遜必侮上。侮上者，逆道也。在人之右，衆必害之。〔一〕霍氏秉權日久，害之者多矣。天下害之，而又行以逆道，不亡何待！」乃上疏言「霍氏泰盛，陛下即愛厚之，宜以時抑制，無使至亡。」書三上，輒報聞。其

後霍氏誅滅，而告霍氏者皆封。人爲徐生上書曰：「臣聞客有過主人者，見其竈直突，傍有積薪，客謂主人，更爲曲突，遠徙其薪，不者且有火患。主人嘿然不應。俄而家果失火，鄰里共救之，幸而得息。於是殺牛置酒，謝其鄰人，灼爛者在於上行，〔二〕餘各以功次坐，而不錄言曲突者。人謂主人曰：『鄉使聽客之言，不費牛酒，終亡火患。〔三〕今論功而請賓，曲突徙薪亡恩澤，燋頭爛額爲上客耶？』主人乃寤而請之。今茂陵徐福數上書言霍氏且有變，宜防絕之。鄉使福說得行，則國亡裂土出爵之費，臣亡逆亂誅滅之敗。往事既已，而福獨不蒙其功，唯陛下察之，貴徙薪曲突之策，使居焦髮灼爛之右。」〔四〕上乃賜福帛十疋，後以爲郎。

〔一〕師古曰：「右，上也。」

〔二〕師古曰：「灼謂被燒炙者也。行音胡（浪）〔郎〕反。」

〔三〕師古曰：「鄉讀曰嚮。次下亦同也。」

〔四〕師古曰：「右，上也。」

宣帝始立，謁見高廟，大將軍光從驂乘，上內嚴憚之，若有芒刺在背。後車騎將軍張安世代光驂乘，天子從容肆體，甚安近焉。〔一〕及光身死而宗族竟誅，故俗傳之曰：「威震主者不畜，霍氏之禍萌於驂乘。」〔二〕

〔一〕師古曰：「肆，放也，展也。近音鉅斳反。」
〔二〕師古曰：「萌謂始生也。」

至成帝時，爲光置守冢百家，吏卒奉祠焉。元始二年，封光從父昆弟曾孫陽爲博陸侯，千戶。

金日磾字翁叔，〔一〕本匈奴休屠王太子也。〔二〕武帝元狩中，票騎將軍霍去病將兵擊匈奴右地，多斬首，虜獲休屠王祭天金人。其夏，票騎復西過居延，攻祁連山，大克獲。於是單于怨昆邪、休屠居西方多爲漢所破，〔三〕召其王欲誅之。昆邪、休屠恐，謀降漢。休屠王後悔，昆邪王殺之，并將其衆降漢。封昆邪王爲列侯。日磾以父不降見殺，與母閼氏、弟倫俱沒入官，輸黃門養馬，時年十四矣。

〔一〕師古曰：「磾音丁奚反。」
〔二〕師古曰：「休音許虯反。屠音儲。」
〔三〕師古曰：「昆音下門反。」

久之，武帝游宴見馬，〔一〕後宮滿側。日磾等數十人牽馬過殿下，莫不竊視，〔二〕至日磾獨不敢。日磾長八尺二寸，容貌甚嚴，馬又肥好，上異而問之，具以本狀對。上奇焉，即日

賜湯沐衣冠，拜爲馬監，遷侍中駙馬都尉光祿大夫。日磾既親近，未嘗有過失，上甚信愛之，賞賜累千金，出則驂乘，入侍左右。貴戚多竊怨，曰：「陛下妄得一胡兒，反貴重之！」上聞，愈厚焉。

〔一〕師古曰：「方於宴游之時，而召閱諸馬。」

〔二〕師古曰：「視宮人。」

日磾母教誨兩子，甚有法度，上聞而嘉之。病死，詔圖畫於甘泉宮，署曰「休屠王閼氏」。〔一〕日磾每見畫常拜，鄉之涕泣，然後乃去。〔二〕日磾子二人皆愛，爲帝弄兒，常在旁側。弄兒或自後擁上項，〔三〕日磾在前，見而目之。〔四〕弄兒走且啼曰：「翁怒。」上謂日磾「何怒吾兒爲？」其後弄兒壯大，不謹，自殿下與宮人戲，日磾適見之，惡其淫亂，遂殺弄兒。弄兒卽日磾長子也。上聞之大怒，日磾頓首謝，具言所以殺弄兒狀。上甚哀，爲之泣，已而心敬日磾。

〔一〕師古曰：「題其畫。」

〔二〕師古曰：「鄉讀曰嚮。」

〔三〕師古曰：「擁，抱也。」

〔四〕師古曰：「目，視怒也。」

初，莽何羅與江充相善，及充敗衛太子，何羅弟通用誅太子時力戰得封。後上知太子

冤，乃夷滅充宗族黨與。何羅兄弟懼及，〔一〕遂謀爲逆。日磾視其志意有非常，心疑之，陰獨察其動靜，與俱上下。〔二〕何羅亦覺日磾意，以故久不得發。是時上行幸林光宮，〔三〕日磾小疾臥廬。〔四〕何羅與通及小弟安成矯制夜出，共殺使者，發兵。明旦，上未起，何羅亡何從外入。〔五〕日磾奏廁心動，〔六〕立入坐內戶下。須臾，何羅褏白刃從東箱上，〔七〕見日磾，色變，走趨臥內欲入，〔八〕行觸寶瑟，僵。日磾得抱何羅，因傳曰：「莽何羅反！」〔九〕上驚起，左右拔刃欲格之，上恐并中日磾，〔一〇〕止勿格。日磾捽胡投何羅殿下，〔一一〕得禽縛之，窮治皆伏辜。繇是著忠孝節。〔一二〕

〔一〕師古曰：「及謂及於禍也。」
〔二〕師古曰：「上下於殿也。」
〔三〕服虔曰：「甘泉一名林光。」師古曰：「秦之林光宮，胡亥所造，漢又於其旁起甘泉宮。」
〔四〕師古曰：「殿中所止曰廬。」
〔五〕師古曰：「無何猶言無故也。」
〔六〕師古曰：「奏，向也。日磾方向廁而心動。」
〔七〕師古曰：「置刃於衣褏中也。褏，古袖字。」
〔八〕師古曰：「趨讀曰趣，嚮也。臥內，天子臥處。」
〔九〕師古曰：「傳謂傳聲而唱之。」

〔一〇〕師古曰：「中音竹仲反。」

〔一一〕孟康曰：「胡音互。捽胡，若今相僻臥輪之類也。」晉灼曰：「胡，頸也，捽其頸而投殿下也。」師古曰：「晉說是也。捽音才乞反。」

〔一二〕師古曰：「繇讀與由同。」

日磾自在左右，目不忤視者數十年。〔一〕賜出宮女，不敢近。上欲內其女後宮，不肯。其篤慎如此，上尤奇異之。〔二〕及上病，屬霍光以輔少主，〔三〕光讓日磾。日磾曰：「臣外國人，且使匈奴輕漢。」於是遂爲光副。光以女妻日磾嗣子賞。初，武帝遺詔以討莽何羅功封日磾爲秺侯，〔四〕日磾以帝少不受封。輔政歲餘，病困，大將軍光白封日磾，臥授印綬。一日，薨，賜葬具冢地，送以輕車介士，軍陳至茂陵，謚曰敬侯。

〔一〕師古曰：「忤，逆也。」

〔二〕師古曰：「篤，厚也。」

〔三〕師古曰：「屬音之欲反。」

〔四〕師古曰：「秺音丁故反。」

日磾兩子，賞、建，俱侍中，與昭帝略同年，共臥起。賞爲奉車、建駙馬都尉。及賞嗣侯，佩兩綬，上謂霍將軍曰：「金氏兄弟兩人不可使俱兩綬邪？」霍光對曰：「賞自嗣父爲侯耳。」上笑曰：「侯不在我與將軍乎？」光曰：「先帝之約，有功乃得封侯。」時年俱八九歲。

宣帝即位，賞爲太僕，霍氏有事萌牙，上書去妻。〔一〕上亦自哀之，獨得不坐。元帝時爲光祿勳，薨，亡子，國除。元始中繼絕世，封建孫當爲秺侯，奉日磾後。

〔一〕師古曰：「萌牙者，言始有端緒，若草之始生。」

初，日磾所將俱降弟倫，字少卿，爲黃門郎，早卒。日磾兩子貴，及孫則衰矣，而倫後嗣遂盛，子安上始貴顯封侯。

安上字子侯，少爲侍中，惇篤有智，宣帝愛之。頗與發舉楚王延壽反謀，〔一〕賜爵關內侯，食邑三百戶。後霍氏反，安上傳禁門闥，無內霍氏親屬，〔二〕封爲都成侯，至建章衞尉。薨，賜冢塋杜陵，謚曰敬侯。四子，常、敞、岑、(哭)〔明〕。

〔一〕師古曰：「與讀曰豫。」

〔二〕師古曰：「禁，止也。門闥，宮中大小之門也。傳聲而止諸門闥也。」

(今)〔岑〕、明皆爲諸曹中郎將，常光祿大夫。元帝爲太子時，敞爲中庶子，幸有寵，帝即位，爲騎都尉光祿大夫，中郎將侍中。元帝崩，故事，近臣皆隨陵爲園郎，敞以世名忠孝，太后詔留侍成帝，爲奉車水衡都尉，至衞尉。敞爲人正直，敢犯顏色，左右憚之，唯上亦難焉。〔一〕病甚，上使使者問所欲，以弟岑爲託。上召岑，拜爲(郎)使主客。〔二〕敞子涉本爲左曹，上拜涉爲侍中，使待幸綠車載送衞尉舍。〔三〕須臾卒。敞三子，涉、參、饒。

〔一〕師古曰：「臣下皆敬憚，唯有天子一人，亦難之。」

〔二〕服虔曰：「官名，屬鴻臚，主胡客也。」

〔三〕李奇曰：「輦綠車，常設以待幸也。臨敞病〔困〕，拜子爲侍中，以此車送，欲敞見其榮寵也。」如淳曰：「幸綠車常置左右以待召載皇孫，今遣涉歸，以皇孫車載之，寵之也。」晉灼曰：「漢注綠車名皇孫車，太子有子乘以從。」師古曰：「如、晉二說是也。」

涉明經儉節，諸儒稱之。成帝時爲侍中騎都尉，領三輔胡越騎。〔一〕哀帝即位，爲奉車都尉，至長信少府。而參使匈奴，匈奴中郎將，〔二〕越騎校尉，關〔內〕都尉，安定、東海太守。饒爲越騎校尉。

〔一〕師古曰：「胡越騎之在三輔者，若長水、長楊、宣曲之屬是也。」

〔二〕師古曰：「以其出使匈奴，故拜爲匈奴中郎將也。」

涉兩子，湯、融，皆侍中諸曹將大夫。〔一〕而涉之從父弟欽舉明經，爲太子門大夫，哀帝即位，爲太中大夫給事中，欽從父弟遷爲尚書令，兄弟用事。帝祖母傅太后崩，欽使護作，〔二〕職辦，擢爲泰山、弘農太守，著威名。平帝即位，徵爲大司馬司直、京兆尹。帝年幼，選置師友，大司徒孔光以明經高行爲孔氏師，京兆尹金欽以家世忠孝爲金氏友。徙光祿大夫侍中，秩中二千石，封都成侯。

〔一〕師古曰：「將亦謂中郎將也。」

〔三〕師古曰：「監主葬送之事也。」

時王莽新誅平帝外家衛氏，召明禮少府宗伯鳳〔一〕入說爲人後之誼，白令公卿、將軍、侍中、朝臣並聽，〔二〕欲以內厲平帝而外塞百姓之議。〔三〕欽與族昆弟秺侯當俱封。初，當曾祖父日磾傳子節侯賞，而欽祖父安上傳子夷侯常，皆亡子，國絕，故莽封欽、當奉其後。當母南即莽母功顯君同產弟也。當上南大行爲太夫人。〔四〕欽因緣謂當：「詔書陳日磾功，亡有賞語。當名爲以孫繼祖也，自當爲父、祖父立廟。〔五〕賞故國君，使大夫主其祭。」〔六〕時甄邯在旁，庭叱欽，〔七〕因劾奏曰：「欽幸得以通經術，超擢侍帷幄，重蒙厚恩，封襲爵號，〔八〕知聖朝以世有爲人後之誼。前遭故定陶太后背本逆天，孝哀不獲厥福，乃者呂寬、衛寶復造姦謀，至於反逆，咸伏厥辜。太皇太后懲艾悼懼，〔九〕逆天之咎，非聖誣法，大亂之殃，誠欲奉承天心，遵明聖制，專壹爲後之誼，以安天下之命，數臨正殿，延見羣臣，講習禮經。孫繼祖者，謂亡正統持重者也。賞見嗣日磾，後成爲君，持大宗重，則禮所謂『尊祖故敬宗』，大宗不可以絕者也。欽自知與當俱拜同誼，即數揚言殿省中，教當云云。〔一○〕當即如其言，則欽亦欲爲父明立廟而不入夷侯常廟矣。進退異言，頗惑衆心，亂國大綱，開禍亂原，誣祖不孝，罪莫大焉。尤非大臣所宜，大不敬。秺侯當上母南爲太夫人，失禮不敬。」莽白太后，下四輔、公卿、大夫、博士、議郎，皆曰：「欽宜以時即罪。」〔一一〕謁者召欽詣詔獄，欽自殺。邯

284 以綱紀國體，亡所阿私，忠孝尤著，益封千戶。更封長信少府涉子右曹湯爲都成侯。湯受
285 封日，不敢還歸家，以明爲人後之誼。益封之後，莽復用欽弟遵，封侯，歷九卿位。

〔一〕如淳曰：「宗伯，姓。」

〔二〕師古曰：「白令皆聽之。」

〔三〕師古曰：「塞，止也。」

〔四〕文穎曰：「南，名也。大行，官名也。當上名狀於大行也。」鄧展曰：「當上南爲太夫人，恃莽姨母故耳。爲父立廟，非也。」

〔五〕晉灼曰：「當是賞弟建之孫，此言自當爲其父及祖父建立廟也。」

〔六〕如淳曰：「以賞故國君，使大夫掌其祭事。」臣瓚曰：「當是支庶上繼大宗，不得顧其外親也。而欽見當母南爲太夫人，遂尊其（祖父）〔父祖〕以續日磾，不復爲後賞，而令大夫主賞祭事。」師古曰：「瓚說是也。」

〔七〕師古曰：「於朝庭中叱之也。」

〔八〕師古曰：「重音直用反。」

〔九〕師古曰：「艾讀曰乂。乂，創也。」

〔一〇〕師古曰：「云云者，多言也。謂上所陳以孫繼祖也。」

〔一一〕師古曰：「卽，就也。」

贊曰：霍光以結髮內侍，起於階闥之間，確然秉志，誼形於主。〔一〕受襁褓之託，任漢室之寄，當廟堂，擁幼君，摧燕王，仆上官，〔二〕因權制敵，以成其忠。處廢置之際，臨大節而不可奪，遂匡國家，安社稷。擁昭立宣，光爲師保，雖周公、阿衡，何以加此！〔三〕然光不學亡術，闇於大理，陰妻邪謀，〔四〕立女爲后，湛溺盈溢之欲，以增顛覆之禍，〔五〕死財三年，宗族誅夷，〔六〕哀哉！昔霍叔封於晉，〔七〕晉卽河東，光豈其苗裔乎？金日磾夷狄亡國，羈虜漢庭，而以篤敬寤主，忠信自著，勒功上將，傳國後嗣，世名忠孝，七世內侍，何其盛也！本以休屠作金人爲祭天主，故因賜姓金氏云。

〔一〕師古曰：「形，見也。」
〔二〕師古曰：「仆，頓也，音赴。」
〔三〕師古曰：「阿衡，伊尹官號也。阿，倚也。衡，平也。言天子所倚，羣下取平也。」
〔四〕晉灼曰：「不揚其過也。」
〔五〕師古曰：「湛讀曰沈。」
〔六〕師古曰：「財與纔同。」
〔七〕師古曰：「霍叔，文王之子，武王之弟也。」

校勘記

二九三二頁九行　光爲奉(常)〔車〕都尉、　景祐、殿、局本都作「車」。

二九三三頁四行　帝(病)〔崩〕，　景祐、殿本都作「崩」。

二九三三頁七行　食邑北海、河〔間〕、東(城)〔郡〕。　齊召南說「河」下脫「間」字，「城」則「郡」之譌，見恩澤侯表。

二九三四頁七行　故欲收(其)〔取〕璽。　景祐、殿本都作「取」。

二九四〇頁五行　(大)〔天〕子所以永保宗廟總壹海內者，　錢大昭說「大」當作「天」。　按景祐、殿、局本都作「天」。

二九四〇頁七行　遣宗正、大鴻臚、光祿大夫奉節使徵昌邑王典喪。服斬縗，〔三〕亡悲哀之心。　錢大昭說，典喪，爲喪主也，顏以「典喪服」爲句，失其指矣。　楊樹達說錢說是，昌邑王傳云「霍光徵王賀典喪」，其明證也。

二九四二頁一六行　直斷(斷)割之而已。　景祐、殿本都不重「斷」字。

二九四七頁九行　(太)〔大〕宗亡嗣，擇支子孫賢者爲嗣。　王念孫說「太宗」當爲「大宗」，各本皆誤。

二九五二頁四行　馮(所謂)〔謂所〕馮者也，　景祐、殿、局本都作「謂所」，此誤倒。

二九五三頁一一行　皆坐逆將軍(竟)〔意〕下獄死。　朱一新說「竟」當爲「意」。　按景祐、殿、局本都作「意」。

二九五四頁二行　輒（使）〔下〕中書令出取之。　景祐、殿本都作「下」。

二九五五頁三行　讙，衆聲也，音（計）〔許〕爰反。　景祐、殿、局本都作「許」，此誤。

二九五六頁九行　光諸女自以（爲）〔於〕上官太后爲姨母，　景祐、殿、局本都作「於」，此誤。

二九五七頁三行　賴（祖宗）〔宗廟〕神靈，　景祐、殿本都作「宗廟」。

二九五八頁一〇行　行音胡（浪）〔郎〕反。　景祐、殿本都作「郎」。

二九六三頁八行　四子，常、敞、岑、（哭）〔明〕。　景祐、殿、局本都作「明」，此誤。

二九六三頁一一行　（今）〔岑〕、明皆爲諸曹中郎將，　景祐、殿、局本都作「岑」，此誤。

二九六三頁一四行　上召岑，拜爲（郎）使主客。　景祐、殿本都無「郎」字。

二九六四頁三行　臨敞病〔困〕，拜子爲侍中，　景祐、殿本都有「困」字。王先謙說有「困」字是。

二九六四頁七行　關〔內〕都尉，　景祐、殿本都有「內」字。宋祁說當刪。

二九六六頁一〇行　遂曾其（祖父）〔父祖〕以續日磾，　景祐、殿本都作「父祖」。

霍光金日磾傳第三十八　漢書六十八

漢　蘭臺令史班固撰

唐正議大夫行秘書少監琅邪縣開國子顏師古注

賜進士出身前翰林院編修國子監祭酒加三級臣王先謙補注

霍光字子孟票騎將軍去病弟也父中孺河東平陽人也師古曰中讀曰仲以縣吏給事平陽侯家師古曰縣遣吏於侯家供事也與侍者衛少兒私通而生去病中孺吏畢歸家娶婦生光因絕不相聞久之少兒女弟子夫得幸於武帝立爲皇后去病以皇后姊子貴幸既壯大迺自知父爲霍中孺未及求問會爲票騎將軍擊匈奴道出河東河東太守郊迎負弩矢先驅師古曰郊迎迎於郊界之上也先驅導其路也至平陽傳舍遣吏迎霍中孺中孺趨入拜謁將軍迎拜因跪曰去病不早自知爲大人遺體也中孺扶服叩頭師古曰服音蒲北反補注先謙曰扶服即匍匐曰老臣得託命將軍此天力也去病大爲中孺買田宅奴婢而去還復過焉乃將光西至長安時年十餘歲任光爲郎稍遷諸曹侍中去病死後光爲奉常都尉光祿大夫補注錢大昭曰常當作車先謙曰官本作車出則奉車入侍左右出入禁闥二十餘年師古曰宮中小門謂之闥小心謹慎未嘗有過甚見親信征和二年衛太子爲江充所敗而燕王旦廣陵王胥皆多過失是時上年老寵姬鉤弋趙倢伃有男師古曰倢伃居鉤弋宮故稱之上心欲以爲嗣命大臣輔之察羣臣唯光任大重可屬社稷師古曰任堪也屬委也任音壬屬音之欲反上迺使黃門畫者畫周公負成王朝諸侯以賜光師古曰黃門之署職任親近以供天子百物在焉故亦有畫工後元二年春上游五柞宮病篤光涕泣問曰如有不諱誰當嗣者師古曰不諱言不可諱也上曰君未諭前畫意邪師古曰諭曉也立少子君行周公之事光頓首讓曰臣不如金日磾日磾亦曰臣外國人不如光上以光爲大司馬大將軍日磾爲車騎將軍及太

僕上官桀爲左將軍搜粟都尉桑弘羊爲御史大夫皆拜臥內牀下師古曰於天子所臥牀前拜職〔補注〕王念孫曰室謂之內故臥室謂之臥內盧綰楚元王傳並云出入臥內周仁傳入臥內史丹傳直入臥內皆是也顏此注及金日磾傳注皆未曉臥內二字之義受遺詔輔少主明日武帝崩太子襲尊號是爲孝昭皇帝帝年八歲政事壹決於光先是後元年侍中僕射莽何羅與弟重合侯通謀爲逆師古曰莽音莫戶反時光與金日磾上官桀等共誅之功未錄武帝病封璽書曰帝崩發書以從事遺詔封金日磾爲秺侯上官桀爲安陽侯光爲博陸侯文穎曰博大陸平取其嘉名無此縣也食邑北海河東城師古曰蓋亦取鄉聚之名以爲國號非必縣也公孫弘平津鄉則是矣〔補注〕齊召南曰注河字下脫間字城則郡之譌恩澤侯表云北海河間東郡師古注光初封食北海河間後益封又食東郡可知此注脫誤顯然先謙曰日磾擒何羅桀光蓋共捕誅通也皆以前捕反者功封時衛尉王莽子男忽侍中師古曰郎右將軍王莽也其子名忽揚語曰師古曰揚謂宣唱之帝病忽常在左右安得遺詔封三子事師古曰安猶焉羣兒自相貴耳光聞之切讓王莽師古曰切深也讓責也

前漢六十八　二

莽酖殺忽〔補注〕先謙曰燕王旦傳蓋主報言獨患光及莽則莽亦重臣也莽字稚叔天水人見公卿表光爲人沈靜詳審長財七尺三寸師古曰財與纔同白晳疏眉目美須頿師古曰晳潔白也頿頰毛也晳音先歷反頿音人占反每出入下殿門止進有常處郎僕射竊識視之不失尺寸師古曰識記也音式志反〔補注〕先謙曰郎有僕射爲諸郎長見百官表其資性端正如此初輔幼主政自己出師古曰自從也天下想聞其風采師古曰采文采殿中嘗有怪一夜羣臣相驚光召尚符璽郎師古曰恐有變難故欲收其璽〔補注〕先謙曰通鑑此句下有欲收取璽四字復引顏注於下是也顏注正釋收璽之故若無四字則召郎語意不完下文郎不肯授無根顏注文義亦無所承各本皆脫賴通鑑存之胡注續志符璽郎中二人在中主璽及虎符竹符之半者官本注其作取郎不肯授光光欲奪之郎按劍曰臣頭可得璽不可得也光甚誼之明日詔增此郎秩二等衆庶莫不多光師古曰多猶重也此事爲多足重也呂光與左將軍桀結婚相親光長女爲桀子安妻有女年與帝相配晉灼曰漢語光嫡妻東閭氏生安夫人昭后之母也桀因帝姊鄂邑蓋主內安女後宮爲倢伃師古曰鄂邑所食邑爲蓋侯所

尚故云蓋主也〔補注〕先謙曰蓋侯王信子充見侯表數月立為皇后父安為票騎將軍封桑
樂侯光時休沐出〔補注〕先謙曰通鑑胡注漢制中朝官五日一下里舍休沐桀輒入代光決事
桀父子既尊盛而德長公主師古曰懷其恩德也公主內行不修近幸河間
丁外人桀安欲為外人求封幸依國家故事以列侯尚公主者光
不許又為外人求光祿大夫欲令得召見又不許長主大以是怨
光而桀安數為外人求官爵弗能得亦慙自先帝時桀已為九卿
位在光右師古曰右上也〔補注〕錢大昕曰公卿表後元二年太僕上官桀為左將軍其初除太僕表不得其年蓋征和二
年公孫敬聲有罪下獄卽以桀代之也先謙曰官本考證云桀為太僕秩中二千石光為奉車都尉僅比二千石故曰位在光右
及父子並為將軍有椒房中宮之重師古曰椒房殿皇后所居皇后親安女光
迺其外祖而顧專制朝事師古曰顧猶反也繇是與光爭權師古曰繇讀與由同燕
王旦自以昭帝兄常懷怨望及御史大夫桑弘羊建造酒榷鹽鐵
為國興利伐其功師古曰伐矜也欲為子弟得官亦怨恨光於是蓋主上

前漢六十八　三

官桀安及弘羊皆與燕王旦通謀詐令人為燕王上書〔補注〕齊召南曰案武
五子傳作旦聞之喜上疏云云則是燕王實使人上書也但下文云調校尉以來未能十日燕王何以得知之又云上書者果亡捕
之甚急則此傳謂蓋主桀安等詐令人為燕王上書正得其實燕刺王傳未及刊正耳先謙曰此正互文見義齊說過泥言光
出都肄郎羽林道上稱蹕孟康曰都試也肄習也師古曰謂總閱試習武備也〔補注〕先謙曰都大總也肄
試習也若今軍營云大操矣省言之則但曰都下文云都郎屬是也孟訓都為試非太官先置師古曰供食飲之具〔補注〕
先謙曰太官掌御飲食有令丞屬少府二事皆言其僭又引蘇武前使匈奴拘留二十年不
降還迺為典屬國〔補注〕先謙曰實十九年而言二十者舉成數也而大將軍長史敞亡功
為搜粟都尉師古曰楊敞也又擅調益莫府校尉師古曰調選也莫府大將軍府也調音徒釣反
光專權自恣疑有非常臣旦願歸符璽入宿衛察姦臣變候司光
出沐日奏之桀欲從中下其事師古曰下謂下有司也音胡稼反〔補注〕先謙曰胡注伺光出沐不在
禁中桀欲自從禁中下其事也桑弘羊當與諸大臣共執退光〔補注〕先謙曰胡注當者以之自任也
書奏帝不肯下明旦光聞之止畫室中不入如淳曰近臣所止計畫之室也或曰彫畫

之室師古曰彫畫是也補注何焯曰畫室郎武帝畫周公負成王朝諸侯以賜光光奉之於室中也沈欽韓曰時蓋已移光祿勳禁止也續志少府屬有畫室署長然則被告劾者待罪之所周壽昌曰畫室當是殿前西閣之室楊敞傳上觀西閣上畫人指桀紂畫謂樂昌侯王武云云又云畫人有堯舜禹湯則知西閣畫古帝王像故稱畫室蔡質漢官典職曰明光殿省中皆以胡粉塗殿紫青界之畫古烈士重行書讚文苑英華盧碩畫諫曰漢文帝於未央宮承明殿畫屈軼草進善旌誹謗木敢諫鼓獬豸益知漢宮殿皆有圖畫也時昭帝御殿內光止西閣之室中以待命不入言不入殿也先謙曰下文光不敢入至殿前而不入也如何說則畫室乃光私室固非沈說移光祿勳禁止此時無詔書亦非桀等所敢出也周說是上問大將軍安在左將軍桀對曰㠯燕王告其罪故不敢入有詔召大將軍光入免冠頓首謝上曰將軍冠師古曰令復著冠也朕知是書詐也將軍亡罪光曰陛下何㠯知之上曰將軍之廣明都郎屬耳師古曰之往也廣明亭名也屬耳近耳也屬音之欲反補注先謙曰耳語詞郎羽林皆郎屬也屬不當訓近胡注廣明亭在長安城東東都門外亦詳戾太子傳調校尉㠯來未能十日燕王何㠯得知之且將軍為非不須校尉文穎曰帝云將軍欲反不由一校尉是時帝年十四尚書左右皆驚補注先謙曰胡注據表尚書中書為兩官續志合為一官此時既有尚書則與中書謁者為兩官明矣沈約宋志亦以為兩官而上書者果亡捕之甚急桀等

前漢六十八 四

懼白上小事不足遂師古曰遂猶竟也不須窮竟也上不聽後桀黨與有譖光者上輒怒曰大將軍忠臣先帝所屬㠯輔朕身師古曰屬委也音之欲反其下亦同敢有毀者坐之自是桀等不敢復言迺謀令長公主置酒請光伏兵格殺之因廢帝迎立燕王為天子事發覺光盡誅桀安弘羊外人宗族燕王蓋主皆自殺光威震海內昭帝既冠遂委任光訖十三年補注先謙曰遂竟也言終委任之訖至也百姓充實四夷賓服元平元年昭帝崩亡嗣武帝六男獨有廣陵王胥在羣臣議所立咸持廣陵王王本㠯行失道先帝所不用光內不自安郎有上書言周太王廢太伯立王季文王舍伯邑考立武王唯在所宜師古曰太伯者王季之兄伯邑考文王長子也雖廢長立少可也廣陵王不可㠯承宗廟言合光意光㠯其書視丞相敞等師古曰視讀曰示敞卽楊敞也擢郎為九江太守卽日承皇太后詔遣行

大鴻臚事少府樂成宗正德光祿大夫吉中郎將利漢迎昌邑王
賀（補注何焯曰史樂成光所親信故首遣之丙吉亦故大將軍長史也）賀者武帝孫昌邑哀王子也
既至即位行淫亂光憂懣（師古曰懣音滿又音悶）獨以問所親故吏大司農
田延年（補注周壽昌曰光爲大將軍在武帝朝無印綬官屬延年初以材略給事大將軍莫府故稱故吏）延年曰
將軍爲國柱石（師古曰柱者梁下之柱石者承柱之礎也言大臣負國重任如屋之柱及其石也）審此人
不可何不建白太后（師古曰立議而白之）更選賢而立之光曰今欲如是於
古嘗有此否（師古曰光不涉學故有此問也補注先謙曰官本否作不）延年曰伊尹相殷廢太
甲以安宗廟後世稱其忠（師古曰商書太甲篇曰太甲既立弗明伊尹放諸桐是也）將軍若能
行此亦漢之伊尹也光迺引延年給事中陰與車騎將軍張安世
圖計（師古曰圖謀也）遂召丞相御史將軍列侯中二千石大夫博士會議
未央宮光曰昌邑王行昏亂恐危社稷如何羣臣皆驚鄂失色（師古
曰凡言鄂者皆謂阻礙不依順也後字作愕其義亦同補注王念孫曰鄂亦驚也若以爲阻礙不依順則上與驚字不相比附下與

前漢六十八　五

失色二字不相連屬矣廣雅愕驚也燕策羣臣驚愕卒起不意盡失其度今人猶曰驚愕曰愕然豈阻礙不依順之謂乎）莫敢
發言但唯唯而已田延年前離席按劍曰先帝屬將軍以幼孤寄
將軍以天下以將軍忠賢能安劉氏也今羣下鼎沸社稷將傾且
漢之傳謚常爲孝者以長有天下（補注宋祁曰孝者下當添所字先謙曰添所字文不順宋說謬）
令宗廟血食也如令漢家絕祀（師古曰如若也）將軍雖死何面目見先帝
于地下乎今日之議不得旋踵（師古曰宜速決）羣臣後應者臣請劍斬之
光謝曰九卿責光是也天下匈匈不安光當受難（師古曰受其憂責也補注宋祁
曰受難改作處難）於是議者皆叩頭曰萬姓之命在於將軍唯大將軍令
（師古曰言一聽之也）光即與羣臣俱見白太后具陳昌邑王不可以承宗廟
狀皇太后迺車駕幸未央承明殿（補注先謙曰胡注未央宮有承明殿天子於是延儒生學士武
帝責莊助曰君厭承明之廬西都賦曰承明金馬著作之庭是也）詔諸禁門毋內昌邑羣臣王入
朝太后還乘輦欲歸溫室（補注先謙曰胡注晉灼云長樂宮有溫室殿黃圖溫室在未央殿北武帝建余

謂長樂周亦有温室但漢諸帝皆居未央則此當爲未央之温室也中黃門宦者各持門扇補注先謙曰中
黃門屬少府黃門令見表王入門閉昌邑羣臣不得入王曰何爲大將軍跪曰
有皇太后詔毋內昌邑羣臣王曰徐之何迺驚人如是光使盡驅
出昌邑羣臣置金馬門外車騎將軍安世將羽林騎收縛二百餘
人皆送廷尉詔獄令故昭帝侍中中臣侍守王補注錢大昭曰侍中爲中朝官故稱
中臣朱一新曰臣當作常先謙曰云守王不須言侍守中臣二字史亦罕見據百官表侍中中常侍皆加官得入禁中則朱說是也
通鑑亦誤作臣光敕左右謹宿衛卒有物故自裁令我負天下有殺主名
師古曰卒讀曰猝物故死也自裁自殺也王尚未自知當廢謂左右我故羣臣從官安
得罪而大將軍盡繫之乎師古曰安焉也補注先謙曰胡注安得罪猶言何所得罪也頊之有
太后詔召王王聞召意恐迺曰我安得罪而召我哉太后被珠襦
如淳曰以珠飾襦也晉灼曰貫珠以爲襦形若今革襦矣師古曰晉說是也盛服坐武帳中侍御數百
人皆持兵期門武士陛戟陳列殿下師古曰陛戟謂執戟以衛陛下也羣臣以次
前漢六十八　六
上殿召昌邑王伏前聽詔光與羣臣連名奏王尚書令讀奏曰丞
相臣敞師古曰楊敞也大司馬大將軍臣光車騎將軍臣安世師古曰張子孺度
遼將軍臣明友師古曰范明友前將軍臣增師古曰韓增後將軍臣充國師古曰趙
充國御史大夫臣誼師古曰蔡誼補注錢大昕曰即蔡義也儒林傳亦作蔡誼案鄭仲師注周禮云古者書儀但爲
義[illegible]今時所謂義爲誼[illegible]漢書項籍傳贊董仲舒傳夏侯勝傳皆以誼爲義義者宜也故字從宜[illegible]宜春侯
臣譚師古曰王訢子當塗侯臣聖師古曰姓魏也隨桃侯臣昌樂師古曰姓趙故蒼梧王趙光子
杜侯臣屠耆堂師古曰故胡人太僕臣延年師古曰杜延年太常臣昌師古曰蒲侯蘇昌
大司農臣延年師古曰田延年宗正臣德師古曰劉向父少府臣樂成師古曰姓史也廷
尉臣光師古曰李光執金吾臣延壽師古曰李延壽大鴻臚臣賢師古曰韋賢左馮
翊臣廣明師古曰田廣明右扶風臣德師古曰周德長信少府臣嘉師古曰不知姓典
屬國臣武師古曰蘇武補注沈欽韓曰容齋四筆武傳昭帝時免武官以故二千石與定策此奏直稱典屬國宣紀封侯
京輔都尉臣廣漢師古曰趙廣漢司隸校尉臣辟兵師古曰不知姓諸吏文
亦然恐誤

學光祿大夫臣遷師古曰王遷臣畸師古曰宋畸臣吉師古曰景吉補注錢大昭曰景吉即丙吉也唐諱丙字故丙丁皆爲景丁臣賜臣管臣勝臣梁臣長幸師古曰並不知姓也臣夏侯勝李奇曰同官同名故以姓別也太中大夫臣德師古曰不知姓臣卬師古曰趙充國子也昧死言皇太后陛下臣敞等頓首死罪天子所㠯永保宗廟總壹海內者補注錢大昭曰大當作天先謙曰官本大作天㠯慈孝禮誼賞罰爲本孝昭皇帝早棄天下亡嗣臣敞等議禮曰爲人後者爲之子也昌邑王宜嗣後遣宗正大鴻臚光祿大夫奉節使徵昌邑王典喪服斬縗師古曰典喪服言爲喪主也斬縗謂縗裳下不緶直斬斬割之而已緶音步千反補注錢大昭曰典喪爲喪主也下言賀服斬縗無悲哀之心顏以典喪服爲句失其指矣先謙曰官本注直下斬字不重胡注引顏删服字亡悲哀之心廢禮誼居道上不素食師古曰素食菜食無肉也言王在道常肉食非居喪之制也而鄭康成解喪服素食云平常之食失之遠矣素食義亦見王莽傳補注沈欽韓曰喪服傳始死至葬朝一溢米夕一溢米既虞食疏食[illegible]水飲既練始食菜果飯素食[illegible]蓋葬前裁令毋絕粒饑死而已既葬始惡食不取飽至練後哀殺乃復其故量取飽而止不飲酒食

前漢六十八　七

肉若侍於尊者亦食之矣通計前後故鄭注素猶故也謂復平生時食也子夏作傳時安知佛法所謂葷素之食顏不當以鄙俗習聞輕詆先儒經訓至此傳稱不素食又別一義管子禁藏篇果蓏素食當十石注果蓏不以火化而食故曰素食墨子辭過篇古之民未知爲飲食時素食而分處然則居喪之禮亦不火食只以糲糗菜果爲膳讀如春秋獻素之素亦不當以釋氏說爲解使從官略女子載衣車內所居傳舍補注先謙曰內與納同始至謁見立爲皇太子補注何焯曰先立爲皇太子則無明世宗不父孝宗之變矣此舊儀不可不素講也常私買雞豚㠯食受皇帝信璽行璽大行前孟康曰漢初有三璽天子之璽自佩行璽信璽在符節臺大行前昭帝柩前也韋昭曰大行不反之辭也就次發璽不封師古曰璽既國器常當緘封而王於大行前受之退還所次遂爾發漏更不封之得令凡人皆見言不重慎也從官更持節師古曰更音工衡反次下亦同引內昌邑從官騶宰官奴二百餘人常與居禁闥內敖戲自之符璽取節十六師古曰之往也自往之署取節也朝暮臨師古曰臨哭臨也音力禁反補注先謙曰官本注奪音字令從官更持節從師古曰更互執節從至哭臨之所爲書曰皇帝問侍中君卿師古曰昌邑之侍中名君卿也使中御府令高昌補注先謙曰百官表御府令屬少府奉黃金千斤賜君卿取十妻大

行在前殿發樂府樂器引內昌邑樂人擊鼓歌吹作俳倡師古曰俳優諧戲也倡樂人也俳音排會下還上前殿如淳曰下謂柩之入冢葬還不居喪位便處前殿也師古曰下音胡稼反擊鐘磬召內泰壹宗廟樂人輦道牟首鄭氏曰祭泰壹神樂人也孟康曰牟首地名也上有觀如淳曰輦道閣道也牟首屏面也以屏面自隔無哀戚也臣瓚曰牟首池名也在上林苑中方在衰絰而輦游於池言無哀戚也師古曰召泰壹樂人內之於輦道牟首而鼓吹歌舞也牟首瓚說是也屏面之言失之遠矣又左思吳都賦云長塗牟首劉逵以爲牟首閣道有室屋也此說更無所出或者思及逵據此輦道牟首便誤用之乎補注劉攽曰輦道輦仁之牟首也䑓下疑予謂牟者岑牟也岑牟蓋鼓角士胄即禰衡爲鼓吏所著者錢大昭曰吳都當作魏魏都注是張孟陽非劉淵林先謙曰言納祀泰壹及祀宗廟之樂人由輦道至牟首爲樂耳牟首似孟說是泰壹見郊祀志鼓吹歌舞悉奏眾樂發長安廚三太牢具祠閣室中如淳曰黃圖北出中門有長安廚故謂之廚城門閣室閣道之有室者不知禱何淫祀也祀已與從官飲啗師古曰啗食也音徒敢反駕法駕皮軒鸞旗驅馳北宮桂宮弄彘鬬虎師古曰皮軒鸞旗皆法駕所陳也北宮桂宮竝在未央宮北補注先謙曰胡注黃圖桂宮武帝造周回十餘里有紫房複道通未央宮三秦記未央宮漸臺西有桂宮先謙案此郎龔遂傳所云召皮軒車九流驅馳東西也召皇太后御

前漢六十八　八

小馬車張晏曰皇太后所駕遊宮中輦車也漢廄有果下馬高三尺以駕輦師古曰小馬可於果樹下乘之故號果下馬補注蘇輿曰黃圖有果馬廄述異記漢樂浪郡有果下馬高三尺魏志穢國出果下馬漢桓帝時獻之使官奴騎乘遊戲掖庭中與孝昭皇帝宮人蒙等淫亂詔掖庭令敢泄言要斬太后曰止師古曰令且止讀奏爲人臣子當悖亂如是邪師古曰責王也悖乖也音布內反王離席伏尚書令復讀曰取諸侯王列侯二千石綬及墨綬黃綬以并佩昌邑郎官者免奴師古曰免奴謂免放爲良人者補注沈欽韓曰御覽五百引新序曰昌邑王治側注之冠十枚以冠賜師友儒者後以冠冠奴龔遂免冠歸之王曰王賜儒者冠下至臣今以餘冠冠奴虜是大王奴虜畜臣也又六百八十二引新序曰龔遂諫云高皇帝造花綬五等陛下取之而與賤人臣以爲不可先謙曰諸綬詳百官表者字當衍變易節上黃旄以赤師古曰以劉屈氂與戾太子戰加節上黃旄遂以爲常賀今輒改之補注沈欽韓曰東京之世皆承用黃旄不敢改至董卓始改赤見袁紹傳注發御府金錢刀劍玉器采繒賞賜所與遊戲者與從官官奴夜飲湛沔於酒師古曰湛讀曰沈又讀曰躭沈沔荒迷也詔太官上乘輿食如故食監奏未釋服未可御故食師古曰釋謂解脫也復詔太官趣

具無關食監師古曰趣讀曰促關由也太官不敢具卽使從官出買雞豚詔殿
門內以爲常師古曰內入也令每日常入雞豚也獨夜設九賓溫室師古曰於溫室中設九賓之禮
也九賓解在叔孫通傳延見姊夫昌邑關內侯祖宗廟祠未舉補注沈欽韓曰未滿既葬
三十六日之制故未祠廟爲璽書使使者持節以三太牢祠昌邑哀王園廟稱
嗣子皇帝師古曰時在喪服故未祠宗廟而私祭昌邑哀王也補注先謙曰胡注賀入繼大宗不當於昌邑哀王稱嗣子
皇帝既於禮悖三年不祭之義又悖爲人後者爲之子之義受璽以來二十七日使者旁午如淳
曰旁午分布也師古曰一從一橫爲旁午猶言交橫也持節詔諸官署徵發凡千一百二十
七事文學光祿大夫夏侯勝等及侍中傅嘉數進諫以過失使人
簿責勝師古曰簿音步戶反簿責以文簿具責之縛嘉繫獄荒淫迷惑失帝王禮誼亂
漢制度臣敞等數進諫不變更師古曰更改也日以益甚恐危社稷天下
不安臣敞等謹與博士臣霸臣雋舍晉灼曰雋姓舍名也下有臣虞舍故以姓別之師古曰雋
音辭阮反又音字阮反臣德臣虞舍臣射臣倉議皆曰高皇帝建功業爲漢

前漢六十八　九

太祖孝文皇帝慈仁節儉爲太宗今陛下嗣孝昭皇帝後行淫辟
不軌師古曰軌法也辟讀曰僻詩云籍曰未知亦既抱子師古曰大雅抑之詩衞武公刺厲王也籍
假也此言假令人云王尚幼少未有所知亦已長大而抱子矣實不幼少也補注先謙曰官本籍作藉案本書藉籍通作五辟
之屬莫大不孝師古曰五辟卽五刑也辟音頻亦反補注先謙曰胡注孝經孔子曰五刑之屬三千其罪莫大於不
孝周襄王不能事母春秋曰天王出居于鄭繇不孝出之絕之於
天下也師古曰襄王惠王子也僖二十四年經書天王出居于鄭公羊傳曰王者無外此其言出何不能乎母也繇讀與由
同宗廟重於君陛下未見命高廟補注先謙曰未見高廟而受命不可以承天序
奉祖宗廟子萬姓當廢臣請有司御史大夫臣誼宗正臣德太常
臣昌與太祝以一太牢具告祠高廟臣敞等昧死以聞皇太后詔
曰可光令王起拜受詔王曰聞天子有爭臣七人雖無道不失天
下師古曰引孝經之言補注沈欽韓曰荀子子道篇作四人家語三恕篇作七人光曰皇太后詔廢安得
天子迺卽持其手師古曰卽就也解脫其璽組奉上太后扶王下殿出金

馬門羣臣隨送王西面拜補注宋祁曰西疑作四先謙曰漢紀通鑑作西曰愚戇不任漢
事起就乘輿副車大將軍光送至昌邑邸補注何焯曰自送至邸防其自裁或他人承望
意指逼之使死致負謗於天下此亦皆光之謹愼也不審其素行於置後之始此則不學爲之光謝曰王行自絕
於天臣等駑怯不能殺身報德臣寧負王不敢負社稷願王自愛
臣長不復見左右師古曰言不復得侍見於左右光涕泣而去羣臣奏言古者廢
放之人屛於遠方不及以政師古曰言不豫政令請徙王賀漢中房陵縣太
后詔歸賀昌邑賜湯沐邑二千戶昌邑羣臣坐亡輔導之誼陷王
於惡光悉誅殺二百餘人出死號呼市中師古曰呼音火故反補注陳景雲曰出死出獄
赴市也又見張敞趙廣漢傳曰當斷不斷反受其亂師古曰悔不早殺光等也補注何焯曰誅其尤無誼
者而流放其餘可也悉誅二百餘人不已濫乎然觀其臨死之言則昌邑羣臣亦謀爲變光微覺之不獨以其行淫亂而憂懣改圖
史家使人得諸言外耳光坐庭中會丞相以下議定所立廣陵王已前不用
及燕剌王反誅其子不在議中近親唯有衛太子孫號皇曾孫在

前漢六十八 十

民間咸稱述焉光遂復與丞相敞等上奏曰禮曰人道親親故尊
祖尊祖故敬宗太宗亡嗣補注王念孫曰太宗當爲大宗各本皆誤王先愼曰宣紀太作大不誤擇
支子孫賢者爲嗣孝武皇帝曾孫病已武帝時有詔掖庭養視至
今年十八師受詩論語孝經躬行節儉補注王先愼曰宣紀躬作操慈仁愛人
可以嗣孝昭皇帝後奉承祖宗廟子萬姓臣昧死以聞皇太后詔
曰可光遣宗正劉德至曾孫家尚冠里洗沐賜御衣補注王念孫曰御衣當爲
御府衣史記李斯傳公子高曰御府之衣臣得賜之中廄之寶馬臣得賜之是也下文云入未央宮見皇太后封爲陽武侯已而光
奉上皇帝璽綬則此時未得遽賜御衣也宣紀正作賜御府衣先謙曰通鑑作御衣蓋承其譌脫太僕以軨獵車
迎曾孫就齋宗正府入未央宮見皇太后封爲陽武侯師古曰解並在宣紀
軨音零已而光奉上皇帝璽綬謁于高廟是爲孝宣皇帝明年下詔
曰夫襃有德賞元功古今通誼也大司馬大將軍光宿衞忠正宣
德明恩守節秉誼以安宗廟其以河北東武陽補注先謙曰河北河東縣在今解州

苪城縣東北一里東武陽東郡縣在曹州府朝城縣西四十里益封光萬七千戶與故所食凡二萬戶賞賜前後黃金七千斤錢六千萬雜繒三萬疋奴婢百七十人馬二千疋甲第一區自昭帝時光子禹及兄孫雲皆中郎將雲弟山奉車都尉侍中領胡越兵光兩女壻為東西宮衞尉(補注)齊召南曰案范明友為未央衞尉鄧廣漢為長樂衞尉昆弟諸壻外孫皆奉朝請為諸曹大夫騎都尉給事中黨親連體根據於朝廷(補注)何焯曰光懲燕王上官之難故使其子孫黨親典兵居中以自衞不思時勢遷變權重勢逼滿盈致禍又基於此不涉學之患也光自後元秉持萬機及上即位迺歸政上謙讓不受諸事皆先關白光然後奏御天子光每朝見上虛己斂容禮下之已甚師古曰下音胡稼反光秉政前後二十年地節二年春病篤車駕自臨問光病上為之涕泣光上書謝恩曰願分國邑三千戶以封兄孫奉車都尉山為列侯奉兄票騎將軍去病祀(補注)先謙曰去病子嬗嗣封薨無後國除故光乞分國邑以奉其祀事下丞相御史即日拜光

前漢六十八　十一

子禹為右將軍光薨上及皇太后親臨光喪太中大夫任宣與侍御史五人持節護喪事中二千石治莫府冢上如淳曰典為冢者賜金錢繒絮繡被百領衣五十篋璧珠璣玉衣師古曰漢儀注以玉為襦如鎧狀連綴之以黃金為縷要已下玉為札長尺廣二寸半為甲下至足亦綴以黃金縷梓宮服虔曰棺也師古曰以梓木為之親身之棺也為天子制故亦稱梓宮便房黃腸題湊各一具服虔曰便房藏中便坐也蘇林曰以柏木黃心致累棺外故曰黃腸木頭皆向內故曰題湊如淳曰漢儀注天子陵中明中高丈二尺四寸周二丈內梓宮次楩椁柏黃腸題湊師古曰便房小曲室也如氏以為楩木名非也(補注)劉攽曰以次言之先親身者衣被次梓宮次便房次題湊次外藏則當以如說為是也且出漢儀注宜以為信爾今但云曲室果何用木為之置於何所耶自是臆說耳宋祁曰小柏室也姚改小曲室也以為梓木姚改以為楩木沈欽韓曰檀弓天子柏椁以端長六尺鄭云以端題湊也正義椁材並皆從下累至上始為題湊湊之嚮也言木之頭相嚮而作四阿也[illegible][illegible]呂覽節喪篇題湊之室高誘注室椁藏也題湊複累棄此為椁之題湊也喪大記注云天子之殯居棺以龍輴欑木題湊象椁上四柱如屋以覆之盡塗之諸侯輴不畫龍欑不題湊象椁其他亦如之此殯之題湊也皆天子之制先謙曰果何用木為之疑作果用何木為之誤倒耳樅木外臧椁十五具服虔曰在正臧外婢妾臧也或曰廚廄之屬也蘇林曰樅木柏

桊松身師古曰爾雅及毛詩傳竝云樅木松葉柏身檜木乃柏葉松身耳蘇說非也樅音七庸反檜音工闊反字亦作栝東園
温明服虔曰東園處此器形如方漆桶開一面漆畫之以鏡置其中以懸屍上大斂竝蓋之師古曰東園署名也屬少府其署
主作此器也〔補注〕王念孫曰案温明下有秘器二字而今本脫之
据服顏二注皆是釋秘器二字後孔光傳光父霸薨賜東園秘器
光薨賜乘輿秘器師古皆無注以注已見於此篇也御覽禮儀部
三十二引此已脫秘器二字文選齊竟陵文宣王行狀注引此正
作東園温明秘器漢紀同[illegible][illegible]皆如乘輿制度載光尸柩以輼輬
車文穎曰輼輬車如今喪轜車也孟康曰如衣車有窗牖閉之則温開之則涼故名之輼輬車也臣瓚曰秦始皇道崩祕其事載
以輼輬車百官奏事如故此不得是轜車類也秦杜延年奏載霍
光柩以輬車駕大廄白虎駟以輼車駕大廄白鹿駟為倅師古曰
輼輬本安車也可以臥息後因載喪飾以柳翣故遂為喪車耳輼
者密閉輬者旁開窗牖各別一乘隨事為名後人既專以載喪又
去其一總為藩飾而合二名呼之耳倅副也音千內反黃屋左纛師古曰解在高紀也發材官輕車北
軍五校士〔補注〕先謙曰百官表虎賁校尉掌輕車中壘校尉掌北軍壘門內外續志中興省中壘但置中候以監五營据
此知西京北軍亦止五營五校即五營也軍陳至茂陵以送其葬〔補注〕沈欽韓曰寰宇記霍光冢在茂平二
陵闕今人耕田時得柏木如塹形謂之柏塹案傳云送至茂陵茂
陵在西安府興平縣東北十七里則光墓當亦在此蓋平陵之西

前漢六十八　十二

茂陵之東謚曰宣成侯發三河卒穿復土起冢祠堂置園邑三百家長
丞奉守如舊法既葬封山為樂平侯以奉車都尉領尚書事天子
思光功德下詔曰〔補注〕宋祁曰此詔紀中已有故大司馬大將軍博陸侯宿衞
孝武皇帝三十有餘年〔補注〕先謙曰官本無有字輔孝昭皇帝十有餘年遭大
難躬秉誼率三公九卿大夫〔補注〕王先慎曰宣紀三公下有諸侯二字定萬世冊以安
社稷〔補注〕先謙曰冊同策天下蒸庶咸以康寧功德茂盛朕甚嘉之復其後
世疇其爵邑應劭曰疇等也師古曰復音方目反世世無有所與功如蕭相國師古曰與
讀曰豫明年夏封太子外祖父許廣漢為平恩侯復下詔曰宣成侯
光宿衞忠正勤勞國家善善及後世師古曰善善者謂褒寵善人也其封光兄孫
中郎將雲為冠陽侯禹既嗣為博陸侯太夫人顯改光時所自造
塋制而侈大之師古曰塋墓域也音營起三出闕築神道北臨昭靈南出承
恩服虔曰昭靈承恩皆館名也李奇曰昭靈高祖母冢園也文穎曰承恩宣平侯冢園也師古曰服說是也文李竝失之盛

飾祠室輦閣通屬永巷而幽良人婢妾守之晉灼曰閣道乃通屬至永巷中也師古曰此亦其家上作輦閣之道及永巷也非謂掖庭之永巷也廣治第室作乘輿輦補注姚鼐曰輦者古人一稱而其制有三者之別詩我任我輦周禮注引司馬法夏后氏謂輦曰余車殷曰胡奴車周曰輜車及左傳輦重如役之輦皆以人輓行重車而大者也小車連車組輓連讀為輦后居宮中從容所乘此則以人輓行輕車而小者也左傳南宮萬以乘車輦其母及魏獻子以二婦人輦以如公國策老婦恃輦而行及此傳乘輿輦皆與巾車連車同制而與輦重之輦異制而雖異而皆有輪皆以人輓行者也至後世帝王游行宮中升降高下又以有輪之輦為不便乃前後皆以人輦之如今之轎無輪唐人謂之擔子亦曰輦王莽傳晉灼注引漢儀注皇后婕妤乘輦輿皆以茵四人舉以行此西都賦乘茵步輦是也言步所以別於有輪之車加畫繡絪馮黃金塗如湻曰絪亦茵馮所謂馮者也以黃金塗飾之師古曰茵蓐也以繡為茵馮而黃金塗輿輦也補注先謙曰官本注所謂作謂所是也與作於引宋祁曰於姚改與韋絮薦輪晉灼曰御輦以韋緣輪著之以絮師古曰取其行安不搖動也著音張呂反侍婢以五采絲輓顯游戲第中師古曰輓謂牽引車輦也音晚初光愛幸監奴馮子都常與計事及顯寡居與子都亂晉灼曰漢語東閭氏亡顯以婢代立素與馮殷姦也師古曰監奴謂奴之監知家務者也殷者子都之名補注周壽昌曰以情事推之疑東閭氏無子僅一女

前漢六十八 十三

為上官安妻顯生子禹故光以為後妻也而禹山亦並繕治第宅走馬馳逐平樂館雲當朝請數稱病私出師古曰請音才姓反多從賓客張圍獵黃山苑中使蒼頭奴上朝謁文穎曰朝當用謁不自行而令奴上謁者也師古曰上謁若今參見尊貴而通名也補注何焯曰上謁猶今鴻臚所收職名先謙曰黃山見東方朔傳莫敢譴者而顯及諸女晝夜出入長信宮殿中亡期度師古曰長信宮上官太后所居宣帝自在民間聞知霍氏尊盛日久內不能善光薨上始躬親朝政御史大夫魏相給事中顯謂禹雲山女曹不務奉大將軍餘業師古曰女音汝曹輩也今大夫給事中他人壹間女能復自救邪師古曰間音居莧反後兩家奴爭道師古曰謂霍氏及御史家霍氏奴入御史府欲蹋大夫門補注先謙曰蹋與踏同御史為叩頭謝迺去人已謂霍氏師古曰告語也顯等始知憂會魏大夫為丞相數燕見言事平恩侯與侍中金安上等徑出入省中時霍山自若領尚書師古曰自若猶言如故也上令吏民得奏封事不關尚書補注何焯曰上下之情通則權復歸王室羣臣進見獨

往來師古曰謂各各得盡言於上也於是霍氏甚惡之宣帝始立立微時許妃爲皇后補注先謙曰官本不重立字引宋祁曰微字上別本更有立字顯愛小女成君欲貴之私使乳醫淳于衍行毒藥殺許后師古曰乳醫視產乳之疾者乳音而樹反補注錢大昭曰宣紀作女侍醫因勸光內成君代立爲后語在外戚傳始許后暴崩吏捕諸醫劾衍侍疾亡狀不道下獄吏簿問急師古曰簿音步戶反顯恐事敗即具以實語光光大驚補注宋祁曰語疑作告欲自發舉不忍猶與師古曰猶與不決也與讀曰豫會奏上因署衍勿論師古曰署者題其奏後也補注齊召南曰案外戚傳同此文注李奇曰光題其奏也師古曰言之於帝故解釋耳光不自署也二注並出師古之手而判然不同胡三省云光薨後帝始聞毒許后事光於是時安敢言於帝耶李奇說是也光薨後語稍泄補注宋祁曰稍下疑有漏字於是上始聞之而未察師古曰未知其虛實迺徙光女婿度遼將軍未央衞尉平陵侯范明友爲光祿勳次婿諸吏中郎將羽林監任勝出爲安定太守補注宋祁曰次字下當有女字數月復出光姊婿給事中光祿大夫張朔爲蜀郡太守羣孫婿中郎

前漢六十八　十四

將王漢爲武威太守頃之復徙光長女婿長樂衞尉鄧廣漢爲少府補注錢大昭曰此少府是長信少府見本紀更以禹爲大司馬冠小冠補注先謙曰胡注大司馬大將軍冠武弁大冠今貶禹故使冠小冠亡印綬罷其右將軍屯兵官屬特使禹官名與光俱大司馬者蘇林曰特但也補注宋祁曰使禹官名字刪官字名下當添爲字先謙曰通鑑亦無爲字又收范明友度遼將軍印綬但爲光祿勳及光中女婿趙平爲散騎騎都尉光祿大夫將屯兵又收平騎都尉印綬諸領胡越騎羽林及兩宮衞將屯兵悉易以所親信許史子弟代之補注何焯曰先收其兵權禹爲大司馬稱病禹故長史任宣候問補注周壽昌曰此禹爲右將軍時之長史也大司馬無官屬宣即前太中大夫護喪事者禹曰我何病縣官非我家將軍不得至是如淳曰縣官謂天子今將軍墳墓未乾盡外我家師古曰外謂疏斥之反任許史奪我印綬補注周壽昌曰右將軍金印紫綬禹拜右將軍至是罷職但領大司馬虛銜令人不省死師古曰不自省有過也補注先謙曰官本注也作耳宣見禹恨望深師古曰望怨也迺謂曰大將軍時何可復行師古

（日言今何得復如此也）持國權柄殺生在手中廷尉李种王平（師古曰种音沖補注先謙曰官本考證云李种公卿表作李仲字季主雒陽人始元元年為廷尉王平徐仁賈勝胡事詳杜延年傳）左馮翊賈勝胡及車丞相女壻少府徐仁（補注周壽昌曰仁字中孫）皆坐逆將軍竟下獄死（補注朱一新曰竟當作意先謙曰官本作意是）使樂成小家子得幸將軍至九卿封侯（師古曰即上所云少府樂成者也使者其姓也字或作史補注周壽昌曰使疑史之誤表作便樂成則又因與使字近而誤）百官以下但事馮子都王子方等（服虔曰皆光奴）視丞相亡如也（師古曰亡如猶如無所象似也補注王念孫曰師古之說甚迂亡如猶云蔑如言百官以下皆蔑視丞相也東方朔傳贊其流風遺書蔑如也蔑與亡一聲之轉史記范雎傳索隱亡猶輕蔑也宣元六子傳今迺遭命離于惡疾夫子所痛曰蔑之命矣夫論語雍也篇蔑作亡論衡問孔篇又作無無與亡古字通故大雅桑柔傳曰蔑無也）各自有時今許史自天子骨肉貴正宜耳大司馬欲用是怨恨愚以為不可禹默然數日起視事顯及禹山雲自見日侵削數相對啼泣自怨山曰今丞相用事縣官信之盡變易大將軍時法令以公田賦與貧民發揚大將軍過失又諸儒

生多窶人子（師古曰窶貧而無禮音其羽反補注朱一新曰爾雅窶貧也詩北門毛傳窶無禮也疏謂貧窶無可為禮師古加而字義不斷）遠客飢寒喜妄說狂言（師古曰善音許吏反）不避忌諱大將軍常讎之（師古曰言嫉之如仇讎也）今陛下好與諸儒生語人人自使書對事（補注何焯曰對或作封誤也後因上書屏不奏乃上封事耳先謙曰官本對作封通鑑作對）多言我家者嘗有上書言大將軍時主弱臣強專制擅權今其子孫用事昆弟益驕恣恐危宗廟災異數見盡為是也其言絕痛山屏不奏其書後上書者益黠盡奏封事輒使中書令出取之（補注先謙曰官本使作下引宋祁曰輒下添使字）不關尚書（補注何焯曰使中書令出取不關尚書一時以防權臣壅蔽然自此浸任宦豎矣成帝以後政出外家有太后為之內主故宦豎不得橈不然霍顯之後必有五侯十常侍之禍人君權宜之制偶然一用事過隨復舊章乃不至左右近習得以干政耳）益不信人顯曰丞相數言我家獨無罪乎山曰丞相廉正安得罪我家昆弟諸壻多不謹又聞民間讙言霍氏毒殺許皇后（師古曰讙衆聲也音計爰反補注先謙曰官本注計作許）寧有是邪顯恐急即具以實告山雲禹山

雲禹驚曰如是何不早告禹等縣官離散斥逐諸壻用是故也此
大事誅罰不小柰何於是始有邪謀矣初趙平客石夏善爲天官
師古曰曉星文者語平曰熒惑守御星御星太僕奉車都尉也不黜則死
平內憂山等雲舅李竟所善張赦見雲家卒卒師古曰卒讀曰猝忽遽之貌也謂
竟曰今丞相與平恩侯用事可令太夫人言太后先誅此兩人移
徙陛下在太后耳長安男子張章告之補注何焯曰褚先生建元以來侯者年表後續記云
張章故潁川人爲長安亭長失官之北闕上書寄宿霍氏第舍臥馬櫪閒夜聞養馬奴相與語言霍氏子孫欲謀反狀因上書告反
事下廷尉執金吾捕張赦石夏等後有詔止勿捕山等愈恐相謂
曰此縣官重太后故不竟也師古曰重難也竟窮竟其事也然惡端已見又有弒
許后事陛下雖寬仁恐左右不聽久之猶發發即族矣不如先也
師古曰言先反遂令諸女各歸報其夫皆曰安所相避師古曰言無處相避當受禍也會
李竟坐與諸侯王交通辭語及霍氏有詔雲山不宜宿衛免就第

前漢六十八 夫

光諸女遇太后無禮服虔曰光諸女自以爲上官太后爲姨母遇之無禮補注先謙曰官本注以下爲作於是
馮子都數犯法上并以爲讓師古曰總以此事責之也山禹等甚恐顯夢第中
井水溢流庭下竈居樹上又夢大將軍謂顯曰知捕兒不師古曰知兒見
補否亟下捕之蘇林曰且疾下捕之師古曰亟音居力反補注先謙曰官本注且作亟第中鼠暴多與
人相觸以尾畫地鴞數鳴殿前樹上師古曰鴞惡聲之鳥也古者室屋高大則通呼爲殿耳非
止天子宮中其語亦見黃霸傳鴞音羽驕反補注先謙曰官本注止作正引宋祁曰正天子姚改止天子第門自壞雲
尙冠里宅中門亦壞巷端人共見有人居雲屋上徹瓦投地就視
亡有大怪之禹夢車騎聲正讙來捕禹舉家憂愁山曰丞相擅減
宗廟羔菟鼃如淳曰高后時定令敢有擅議宗廟者棄市師古曰羔菟鼃所以供祭也可以此罪也謀
令太后爲博平君置酒文穎曰宣帝外祖母也召丞相平恩侯以下使范明
友鄧廣漢承太后制引斬之因廢天子而立禹約定未發雲拜爲
玄菟太守太中大夫任宣爲代郡太守山又坐寫祕書顯爲上書

獄城西第入馬千匹以贖山罪書報聞師古曰不許之會事發覺雲山明友自殺顯禹廣漢等捕得禹要斬顯及諸女昆弟皆弃市唯獨霍后廢處昭臺宮與霍氏相連坐誅滅者數千家補注先謙曰此言其株連之多通鑑作數十疑非上迺下詔曰迺者東織室令史張赦使魏郡豪李竟報冠陽侯雲謀為大逆師古曰解在宣紀也朕以大將軍故抑而不揚冀其自新今大司馬博陸侯禹與母宣成侯夫人顯及從昆弟子冠陽侯雲樂平侯山諸姊妹壻謀為大逆欲詿誤百姓賴祖宗神靈補注先謙曰祖宗官本作宗廟先發得咸伏其辜師古曰事發而捕得朕甚悼之諸為霍氏所詿誤事在丙申前未發覺在吏者皆赦除之男子張章先發覺以語期門董忠忠告左曹楊惲惲告侍中金安上惲召見對狀後章上書以聞侍中史高與金安上建發其事師古曰言共立意發之也言無入霍氏禁闥卒不得遂其謀師古曰遂成也皆讎有功晉灼曰讎等也師古曰言其功相等類也補注先謙曰顧炎武云注非也此如詩無言不讎之讎左傳憂必讎焉注讎猶對也律歷志廣延宣問以理星度未能讎之讎也郊祀志其方盡多不讎伍被傳忠不終而詐讎魏其傳上使御史簿責嬰所言頗不讎王念孫云晉說是也爾雅讎匹也廣雅等匹讎輩也與晉說讎等義一而已召誥敢以王之讎民百君子是讎為相等之義也此言張章諸人皆讎有功則讎當訓為等不當訓為對故師古曰言其功相等類也若詩之無言不讎左傳之憂必讎焉則與此訓為等者異義至所引律歷志以下諸條則去此益遠矣

前漢六十八 七

封章為博成侯忠高昌侯惲平通侯安上都成侯高樂陵侯初霍氏奢侈茂陵徐生曰霍氏必亡夫奢則不遜不遜必侮上侮上者逆道也在人之右眾必害之師古曰右上也霍氏秉權日久害之者多矣天下害之而又行以逆道不亡何待迺上疏言霍氏泰盛陛下即愛厚之宜以時抑制無使至亡書三上輒報聞其後霍氏誅滅而告霍氏者皆封人為徐生上書曰臣聞客有過主人者見其竈直突傍有積薪補注何焯曰突當為窔式林反與窔字異義玉篇所分甚明客謂主人更為曲突遠徙其薪補注沈欽韓曰淮南說山訓湻于髡之告失火高誘注湻于髡告其鄰使曲突徙薪鄰人不從後竟失火言者不為功焦

頭爛額為上客不者且有火患主人嘿然不應俄而家果失火鄰里共救
之幸而得息於是殺牛置酒謝其鄰人灼爛者在於上行師古曰灼謂被
燒炙者也行音胡浪反補注先謙曰浪官本作郎餘各以功次坐而不錄言曲突者人謂
主人曰鄉使聽客之言不費牛酒終亡火患師古曰鄉讀曰嚮次下亦同也今論
功而請賓曲突徙薪亡恩澤燋頭爛額為上客耶主人迺寤而請
之今茂陵徐福數上書言霍氏且有變宜防絕之鄉使福說得行
則國亡裂土出爵之費臣亡逆亂誅滅之敗往事既已而福獨不
蒙其功唯陛下察之貴徙薪曲突之策使居焦髮灼爛之右師古曰右上也
上迺賜福帛十疋補注王念孫曰告霍氏者皆封侯而徐福僅賜帛十匹則輕重相去太遠十匹當為千匹
通鑑作十匹則所見漢書本已誤御覽居處部十四治道部十四引此並作千匹漢紀同後以為郎宣帝始立
謁見高廟大將軍光從驂乘補注先謙曰胡注漢制大駕大將軍驂乘上內嚴憚之若
有芒刺在背後車騎將軍張安世代光驂乘天子從容肆體甚安
近焉師古曰肆放也展也近音鉅靳反 前漢六十八 十六 及光身死而宗族竟誅故俗傳之曰威震
主者不畜霍氏之禍萌於驂乘師古曰萌謂始生也至成帝時為光置守冢
百家吏卒奉祠焉元始二年封光從父昆弟曾孫陽為博陸侯千
戶

金日磾字翁叔師古曰磾音丁奚反本匈奴休屠王太子也師古曰休音許虯反屠音儲
武帝元狩中票騎將軍霍去病將兵擊匈奴右地多斬首虜獲休
屠王祭天金人補注宋祁曰去病傳作天祭金人其夏票騎復西過居延攻祁連
山大克獲於是單于怨昆邪休屠居西方多為漢所破師古曰昆音下門反
召其王欲誅之昆邪休屠恐謀降漢休屠王後悔昆邪王殺之并
將其眾降漢封昆邪王為列侯日磾以父不降見殺與母閼氏弟
倫俱沒入官輸黃門養馬時年十四矣久之武帝游宴見馬師古曰方
於宴游之時而召閱諸馬後宮滿側日磾等數十人牽馬過殿下莫不竊視師古

曰視宮人至日磾獨不敢日磾長八尺二寸容貌甚嚴馬又肥好上異
而問之具以本狀對上奇焉卽日賜湯沐衣冠拜爲馬監遷侍中
駙馬都尉光祿大夫日磾既親近未嘗有過失上甚信愛之賞賜
累千金出則驂乘入侍左右貴戚多竊怨曰陛下妄得一胡兒反
貴重之上聞愈厚焉日磾母教誨兩子甚有法度上聞而嘉之病
死補注宋祁曰病疑作母詔圖畫於甘泉宮署曰休屠王閼氏師古曰題其畫日磾
每見畫常拜鄉之涕泣然後迺去師古曰鄉讀曰嚮日磾子二人皆愛爲
帝弄兒常在旁側補注王先愼曰旁卽側也二字不當連文疑旁是帝形近而誤弄兒或自後擁
上項師古曰擁抱也日磾在前見而目之師古曰目視怒也弄兒走且啼曰翁怒
上謂日磾何怒吾兒爲其後弄兒壯大不謹自殿下與宮人戲日
磾適見之惡其淫亂遂殺弄兒弄兒卽日磾長子也上聞之大怒
日磾頓首謝具言所以殺弄兒狀上甚哀爲之泣已而心敬日磾

初莽何羅與江充相善及充敗衛太子何羅弟通用誅太子時力
戰得封後上知太子冤迺夷滅充宗族黨與何羅兄弟懼及師古曰及[illegible]誅及於
禍也遂謀爲逆日磾視其志意有非常心疑之陰獨察其動靜
與俱上下師古曰上下於殿也何羅亦覺日磾意以故久不得發是時上行
幸林光宮服虔曰甘泉一名林光師古曰秦之林光宮胡亥所造漢又於其旁起甘泉宮日磾小疾臥廬
師古曰殿中所止曰廬何羅與通及小弟安成矯制夜出共殺使者發兵明
旦上未起補注王念孫曰案未起上脫臥字通鑑無臥字則所見漢書本已然文選西征賦注御覽人事部五十八引此
並作上臥未起漢紀同何羅亡何從外入師古曰無何猶言無故也日磾奏廁心動師古曰奏
向也日磾方向廁而心動立入坐內戶下補注先謙曰內房也坐殿房之戶下以俟之或據御覽四百十七引作臥
內以爲坐當作臥但上之臥內日磾何敢遽入且何羅見日磾在臥內無反趨臥內欲入之理御覽未足據也如此文作臥內顏解
臥內之義不應在下知所見本亦作坐不作臥也須臾何羅褎白刃從東箱上師古曰直刃於衣褎
中也褎古袖字見日磾色變走趨臥內欲入師古曰趨讀曰趣嚮也臥內天子臥處補注先謙曰臥內

卽臥室詳見上行觸寶瑟僵日磾得抱何羅因傳曰莽何羅反師古曰傳謂傳聲而唱之上驚起左右拔刃欲格之上恐并中日磾師古曰中音竹仲反止勿格日磾捽胡投何羅殿下孟康曰胡音互捽胡若今相僻卧輪之類也晉灼曰胡頸也捽其頸而投殿下也師古曰晉說是也捽音才乞反補注宋祁曰卧輪當改卧輪沈欽韓曰釋名胡互也在咽下垂能歛互物也先謙曰官本注乞作兀得禽縛之窮治皆伏辜繇是著忠孝節師古曰繇讀與由同日磾自在左右目不忤視者數十年師古曰忤逆也賜出宮女不敢近上欲內其女後宮不肯其篤慎如此上尤奇異之師古曰篤厚也及上病屬霍光以輔少主師古曰屬音之欲反補注宋祁曰及上下當添疾字光讓日磾日磾曰臣外國人且使匈奴輕漢於是遂爲光副補注齊召南曰案與霍光同傳故彖其文不言拜爲車騎將軍也光以女妻日磾嗣子賞初武帝遺詔以討莽何羅功封日磾爲秺侯師古曰秺音丁故反補注沈欽韓曰說文作㾴云濟陰有㾴縣明志兗州府城武縣南有廢秺縣日磾以帝少不受封補注何焯曰以帝少不受封安得來王忽自相貴之謗大將軍識不逮也輔政歲餘病困大將軍光白封日

前漢六十八 廿

磾臥授印綬一日薨賜葬具冢地送以輕車介士軍陳至茂陵諡曰敬侯日磾兩子賞建俱侍中與昭帝略同年共臥起賞爲奉車補注王念孫曰奉車下亦有都尉二字而今本脫之百官表云奉車都尉掌御乘輿車駙馬都尉掌駙馬藝文類聚人部十七御覽儀式部三引此並作賞爲奉車都尉建駙馬都尉建駙馬都尉及賞嗣侯佩兩綬上謂霍將軍曰金氏兄弟兩人不可使俱兩綬邪霍光對曰賞自嗣父爲侯耳上笑曰侯不在我與將軍乎光曰先帝之約有功迺得封侯時年俱八九歲宣帝卽位賞爲太僕霍氏有事萌芽上書去妻師古曰萌芽者言始有端緖若草之始生補注錢大昕曰案公卿表宣帝甘露四年秺侯金賞爲侍中太僕距霍氏之亡已十六年矣霍氏有事之始賞祇爲侍中未任太僕也王文彬曰賞去妻乃作筆不必與上爲太僕連文錢說過泥先謙曰官本芽作牙上亦自哀之獨得不坐元帝時爲光祿勳薨亡子國除元始中繼絕世封建孫當爲秺侯奉日磾後初日磾所將俱降弟倫字少卿爲黃門郎早卒日磾兩子貴及孫則衰矣而倫後嗣遂盛子安上始貴

顯封侯

安上〔補注〕先謙曰官本並與上連文字子侯少爲侍中惇篤有智宣帝愛之頗與

發舉楚王延壽反謀師古曰與讀曰豫賜爵關內侯食邑三百戶後霍氏

反安上傳禁門闥無內霍氏親屬師古曰禁止也門闥宮中大小之門也傳聲而止諸門闥也

封爲都成侯至建章衛尉薨賜冢塋杜陵諡曰敬侯四子常敞岑

哭今明〔補注〕錢大昭曰哭今當作明岑南監本閩本皆不誤先謙曰官本不誤皆爲諸曹中郎將常

光祿大夫元帝爲太子時敞爲中庶子幸有寵帝即位爲騎都尉

光祿大夫中郎將侍中元帝崩故事近臣皆隨陵爲園郎敞以世

名忠孝太后詔留侍成帝爲奉車水衡都尉〔補注〕錢大昭曰百官表奉車都尉掌御乘

輿車水衡都尉掌上林苑此云奉車水衡都尉當是先後任此兩職不重言都尉者省文也至衛尉〔補注〕先謙曰敞以成

帝河平四年由侍中奉車都尉爲水衡次年陽朔元年爲衛尉見公卿表敞爲人正直敢犯顏色左右

憚之唯上亦難焉師古曰臣下皆敬憚唯有天子一人亦難之〔補注〕先謙曰唯與雖同言不獨左右憚之雖上亦

前漢六十八　二十

難之也顏訓誤詳見韓信傳病甚上使使者問所欲以弟岑爲託上召岑拜爲

郎使主客師古曰官名屬鴻臚主胡客也〔補注〕先謙曰官本召作詔無郎字引宋祁曰拜爲下當添郎字錢大昕云百官

表大鴻臚屬無此官敞子涉本爲左曹上拜涉爲侍中使待幸綠車載送衛

尉舍李奇曰輦綠車常設以待幸也臨敞病拜子爲侍中以此車送欲敞見其榮寵也如淳曰幸綠車常置左右以待召載皇

孫今遣涉歸以皇孫車載之寵之也晉灼曰漢注綠車名皇孫車太子有子乘以從師古曰如晉二說是也〔補注〕周壽昌曰續志皇

孫綠車如云幸綠車不成文義先謙曰官本病下有困字是須臾卒〔補注〕先謙曰據表敞卒於陽朔四年敞三子

涉參饒涉明經儉節諸儒稱之成帝時爲侍中騎都尉領三輔胡

越騎師古曰胡越騎之在三輔者若長水長楊宣曲之屬是也哀帝即位爲奉車都尉至長信

少府而參使匈奴匈奴中郎將師古曰以其出使匈奴故拜爲匈奴中郎將也〔補注〕周壽昌曰使匈

奴下應有拜字各本俱脫惟凌本有宜從之越騎校尉關都尉〔補注〕先謙曰官本作關內都尉引宋祁曰當刪

內字安定東海太守饒爲越騎校尉涉兩子湯融皆侍中諸曹將大

夫師古曰將亦謂中郎將也〔補注〕先謙曰將大夫之稱亦見百官表而涉之從父弟欽舉明經爲

太子門大夫補注先謙曰門大夫亦太子太傅少傅屬官哀帝即位爲太中大夫給事中欽從父弟遷爲尚書令兄弟用事帝祖母傅太后崩欽使護作師古曰監主葬送之事也補注王文彬曰欽使疑當作使欽職辦擢爲泰山弘農太守著威名平帝即位徵爲大司徒司直補注周壽昌曰一本作大司馬案哀帝時更丞相爲大司徒丞相有司直大司馬位雖尊於元壽二年始置官屬有長史不聞有司直也先謙曰官本作大司馬京兆尹帝年幼選置師友大司徒孔光以明經高行爲孔氏師京兆尹金欽以家世忠孝爲金氏友徙光祿大夫侍中秩中二千石封都成侯時王莽新誅平帝外家衛氏召明禮少府宗伯鳳如淳曰宗伯姓補注先謙曰鳳字君房見表入說爲人後之誼白令公卿將軍侍中朝臣並聽師古曰白令皆聽之欲以內厲平帝而外塞百姓之議師古曰塞止也欽與族昆弟秺侯當俱封初當曾祖父日磾傳子節侯賞補注錢大昕曰功臣表失載賞謚而欽祖父安上傳子夷侯常皆亡子國絕故莽封欽當奉其後當母南即莽母功顯君

前漢六十八　圭

同產弟也當上南大行爲太夫人文穎曰南名也大行官名也當上名狀於大行也鄧展曰當上南爲太夫人特莽姨母故耳爲父立廟非也補注先謙曰官本注官名下無也字欽因緣謂當詔書陳日磾功亡有賞語當名爲以孫繼祖也自當爲父祖父立廟晉灼曰當是賞弟建之孫此言自當爲其父及祖父建立廟也賞故國君使大夫主其祭如淳曰以賞故國君使大夫掌其祭事臣瓚曰當是支庶上繼大宗不得顧其外親也而欽見當母南爲太夫人遂尊其祖父以續日磾不復爲後賞而令大夫主賞祭事師古曰瓚說是也補注先謙曰官本祖父作父祖時甄邯在旁庭叱欽師古曰於朝庭中叱之也因劾奏曰欽幸得以通經術超擢侍帷幄重蒙厚恩封襲爵號師古曰重音直用反知聖朝以世有爲人後之誼前遭故定陶太后背本逆天孝哀不獲厥福迺者呂寬衛寶復造姦謀至於反逆咸服厥辜太皇太后懲艾悼懼師古曰艾讀曰乂乂創也逆天之咎非聖誣法大亂之殃誠欲奉承天心遵明聖制專壹爲後之誼以安天下之命數臨正殿延見羣臣講習禮經孫繼祖者謂亡正統持重者也賞見嗣日磾後

成爲君持大宗重（補注先謙曰官本後作從引宋祁曰從成姚本作後成）則禮所謂尊祖故敬宗大宗不可以絕者也欽自知與當俱拜同誼卽數揚言殿省中敎當云云（師古曰云云者多言也謂上所陳以孫繼祖也）當卽如其言則欽亦欲爲父明立廟而不入夷侯常廟矣進退異言頗惑衆心（補注宋祁曰頗惑當作疑惑）亂國大綱開禍亂原誣祖不孝罪莫大焉尤非大臣所宜大不敬秺侯當上母南爲太夫人失禮不敬莽白太后下四輔公卿大夫博士議郎皆曰欽宜以時卽罪（師古曰卽就也）謁者召欽詣詔獄欽自殺邯以綱紀國體亡所阿私忠孝尤著益封千戶更封長信少府涉子右曹湯爲都成侯湯受封日不敢還歸家以明爲人後之誼益封之後莽復用欽弟遵封侯歷九卿位

虛受堂

贊曰霍光以結髮內侍起於階闥之間確然秉志誼形於主（師古曰形見也）受襁褓之託任漢室之寄當廟堂擁幼君摧燕王仆上官（師古曰仆頓也音赴）因權制敵以成其忠處廢置之際臨大節而不可奪遂匡國家安社稷擁昭立宣光爲師保雖周公阿衡何以加此（師古曰阿衡伊尹官號也阿倚也衡平也言天下所倚挈以取平也）然光不學亡術闇於大理陰妻邪謀（晉灼曰不揚其過也）立女爲后湛溺盈溢之欲以增顛覆之禍（師古曰湛讀曰沈）死財三年宗族誅夷（師古曰財與纔同）哀哉昔霍叔封於晉（師古曰霍叔文王之子武王之弟也補注何焯曰昭宣之際有推霍光爲霍叔後者其語殊謬足累光之誠節詳見史記三代世表後褚少孫所記班氏特畧舉於贊中以傳疑亦兼以爲儆戒云）晉卽河東光豈其苗裔乎金日磾夷狄亡國羈虜漢庭而以篤敬寤主忠信自著勒功上將傳國後嗣世名忠孝七世內侍何其盛也本以休屠作金人爲祭天主故因賜姓金氏云

霍光金日磾傳第三十八　終

漢書六十八